SONGBIRDS

SONGBIRDS

Celebrating Nature's Voices

RONALD ORENSTEIN

KEY PORTER BOOKS

Gratefully dedicated to Dr. J. Murray Speirs

page 1: A Wood Thrush nest, with interlopers. The three blue eggs belong to the thrush; the two speckled eggs were laid by Brown-headed Cowbirds.

page 3: An American Robin plucks a mountain ash berry.

Copyright © 1997 by Ronald Orenstein

Canadian Cataloguing in Publication Data

Orenstein, Ronald I. (Ronald Isaac), 1946-
Songbirds : celebrating nature's voices

Includes index.
ISBN 1-55013-881-2

1. Songbirds. 2. Songbirds-Pictorial works. I. Title.

QL674.O73   1997   598.8   C97-931219-1

The publisher gratefully acknowledges the support of the Canada Council for the Arts and the Ontario Arts Council for its publishing program.

Key Porter Books Limited
70 The Esplanade
Toronto, Ontario
Canada M5E 1R2

THE CANADA COUNCIL | LE CONSEIL DES ARTS
FOR THE ARTS | DU CANADA
SINCE 1957 | DEPUIS 1957

Design: Scott Richardson
Electronic formatting: Leah Gryfe

Printed and bound in Canada

97 98 99 00 6 5 4 3 2 1

Photography Credits

Page 1: © T. Fink/VIREO; 3: © Mark F. Wallner/Wing It Wildlife; 7: © Frithfoto/Bruce Coleman Inc.; 11: © V. Hasselblad/VIREO; 13: © Wayne Lynch; 14: © Marie Read; 16: © M. F. Soper/A.N.T. Photo Library; 19: © D. Wechsler/VIREO; 20: © W. Peckover/VIREO; 22: © G. Lasley/VIREO; 23: © L & O Schick/Nature Focus; 24: © Jack Jeffrey; 31: © Horst Mueller/VIREO; 32 (left): © A. Morris/VIREO; 32 (right): © Joe McDonald/Bruce Coleman Inc.; 34: © T. J. Ulrich/VIREO; 35: © D. Wechsler/VIREO; 37: © F. Lane/Bruce Coleman Inc.; 39: © Michael Fogden/Bruce Coleman Inc.; 40: © Nature Focus/T. & P. Gardner; 42: © Len Robinson/Bruce Coleman Inc.; 43: © W. Peckover/VIREO; 44: © R.Garstone/Nature Focus; 46: © Rick & Nora Bowers/VIREO; 49: © J. R. Woodward/VIREO; 57: © Michael Morcombe/Bruce Coleman Inc.; 58: © Bill Marchel; 61: © A.& E. Morris/ VIREO; 64: © Des & Jen Bartlett/Bruce Coleman Inc.; 65: © A. Morris/VIREO; 68: © Brian J. Coates/A.N.T. Photo Library; 70: © Marie Read; 71: © Don Hadden/VIREO; 73: © Don Hadden/VIREO; 77: © Steven Holt/VIREO; 78: © W. Peckover/VIREO; 79: Johann Schumacher Design; 82: © Bill Marchel; 85: © D. Wechsler/VIREO; 86: © Bill Marchel; 89: © Frithfoto/Bruce Coleman Inc.; 90: © Brian J. Coates/Bruce Coleman Inc.; 91 (left): © J. Dunning/VIREO; 91 (right): © Michael Fogden/Bruce Coleman Inc.; 92: © Ralph & Daphne Keller/A.N.T. Photo Library; 93: © Cyril Webster/A.N.T. Photo Library; 99: © Johann Schumacher; 100: © Roger Wilmshurst/Bruce Coleman Inc.; 106: © W. R. Moore/Nature Focus; 109: © Bill Marchel; 110: © R. Chittenden/VIREO; 114: © Marie Read; 115: © Bill Goulet/Bruce Coleman Inc.; 116: © K. Griffiths/A.N.T. Photo Library; 121: © Keith Richards/Nature Focus; 122 © Fletcher & Baylis; 123: © M. Strange/VIREO; 124: © Brian Beck Photography; 125: © Frank Park/A.N.T. Photo Library; 126: © Jen & Des Bartlett/Bruce Coleman Inc.; 127: © A. Walther/VIREO; 128: © Marie Read; 129: © Michael Frye; 134: © Johann Schumacher Design; 136: © Kenneth W. Fink/Bruce Coleman Inc.; 137: © Babs & Bert Wells/Nature Focus; 143: © Marie Read; 144: © Tui De Roy/Bruce Coleman Inc.; 147: © P. Ryan; 149: © Rob Curtis/VIREO; 150: © J. Dunning/VIREO; 151: © Jack Jeffrey; 152: © G. D. Anderson/A.N.T. Photo Library; 153: © Bill Marchel; 154: © P. La Tourrette/VIREO; 155: © J. Dunning/VIREO; 156: © D. Wechsler/VIREO; 159: © J. C. Carton/Bruce Coleman Inc.; 161: © Tui De Roy/Bruce Coleman Inc.; 162: © Peter Davey/Bruce Coleman Inc.; 167: © Bill Marchel; 168: © A. Morris/VIREO; 169: © J. C. Carton/ Bruce Coleman Inc.; 170: © J. Dunning/VIREO; 171: © Joe McDonald/Bruce Coleman Inc.; 174: © Brian Beck Photography; 179: © Tui De Roy/Bruce Coleman Inc.; 180: © Wayne Lynch; 181: © Wayne Lynch; 183: © T. Beck/VIREO; 187: © Eric. A. Soder; 188: © D. Wechsler/VIREO; 192 (left): © J. H. Dick/VIREO; 192 (right): © H. Douglas Pratt; 193: © R.J.Shallenberger; 194: © R. L. Pitman/VIREO; 195: © H. Webster/Nature Focus; 201: © J. R. Woodward/VIREO; 204: © J. Dunning/VIREO; 205: © P. W. Sykes, Jr./VIREO.

CONTENTS

PREFACE

In one moment I've seen what has hitherto been
Enveloped in absolute mystery,
And without extra charge I will give you at large
A Lesson in Natural History...

As to temper the Jubjub's a desperate bird,
Since it lives in perpetual passion:
Its taste in costume is entirely absurd—
It is ages ahead of the fashion.

—LEWIS CARROLL, *The Hunting of the Snark*

This Victoria's Riflebird from north-eastern Australia could be a female or a young male. If it is a male, it may, like many other birds-of-paradise, take years to develop its adult plumage.

I might as well confess it—I am an unrepentant dickey-bird man. Others may prefer the majesty of birds of prey, the beauty of pheasants, the stateliness of cranes, or the charm of ducks and geese, but it is the songbirds that fascinate me. This book is an attempt to share that fascination.

I had better explain what I mean by "songbirds." Strictly speaking, the word should apply only to the "true" songbirds of the Suborder Oscines, perching birds that learn a good portion of their song repertoires. In this book, however, I am using it to cover the entire order Passeriformes, including suboscine birds such as the tyrant flycatchers, cotingas, and pittas. I make no apology for this. The suboscines are simply too interesting to leave out.

I have decided not to include scientific names in the main text of this book. You will find them, with brief notes on distribution, in an appendix at the back. In general, I have followed *Distribution and Taxonomy of Birds of the World* by Charles Sibley and Bert Monroe Jr. as my source for English and scientific names. I have not, however, been slavish about this. I have felt no compunction about departing from Sibley and Monroe for English names when those authors have ignored names widely used by English-speaking birders. Thus, I use "Dunnock" instead of

"Hedge Accentor," and "Bearded Reedling" instead of "Bearded Parrotbill" (which may indicate its nearest relatives but is totally inappropriate for this thin-billed bird) or, for that matter, the more common "Bearded Tit," which is just plain wrong. I have also preferred to give South African birds the English names birders use for them in that country.

English names in the book, following the usual convention in ornithology, are capitalized when they are given in full for a particular species. Thus, "Brown-headed Cowbird" is capitalized but "cowbird," referring to any species in that group, is not.

In writing this book, I have consulted many scientific papers in the recent literature. Because this is not intended to be a scientific text, I have not listed these references in this book. Anyone who would like a list of the papers I consulted can write me at 1825 Shady Creek Court, Mississauga, Ontario, Canada L5L 3W2, or send me e-mail at ornstn@inforamp.net.

I have a number of people to thank before we go on. Barry Kent MacKay was originally to be co-author of this book, but other commitments made that impossible. He was, however, very much involved in planning its original outline, and I am very glad to be able to include some of his art here. Barry, Jessica Speart, and especially Kaaren Dickson, all dear friends, listened patiently as I read portions of the text to them over the telephone. Poor Kaaren had to put up with almost the whole thing, and her comments were extremely encouraging and helpful.

I would like to thank the staff at Key Porter Books, especially my editor, Michael Mouland. Staff at the libraries of the Royal Ontario Museum and the Bird Division, University of Michigan, Ann Arbor, were most helpful. I owe special thanks to Robert B. Payne, Janet Hinshaw, and Robert W. Storer at the University of Michigan. Dr. Payne in particular pointed out some valuable recent references on molt and other topics. I have also benefitted greatly from discussions on the Internet list Birdchat.

Bruce Beehler and J. Bruce Falls answered some thorny questions for me as I wrote. Barry MacKay, Drs. Beehler and Falls, Alan H. Brush, and James D. Rising checked all or part of the manuscript for accuracy, though the responsibility for any errors is my own. Although I did not consult him directly, I owe a particular debt to Dr. Frank Gill for his thorough text *Ornithology*, which provided an invaluable starting point for the research that went into this book.

I also owe a particular debt to the people who taught me ornithology: my graduate supervisors Jon C. Barlow and Robert W. Storer, and especially Dr. J. Murray Speirs, to whom this book is gratefully dedicated. My debt to my parents, Charles and Mary Orenstein, who made it possible for me to see the birds of the world and to pursue their study, is not something I can express adequately here. Finally, I would like to thank my children, Randy and Jenny, for putting up with my lack of attention, while I toiled away on this book, with (more or less) good grace, and who have submitted to being dragged off on birding trips without (too much) complaining.

ONE

WHAT IS A SONGBIRD?

… The lords of creation

are in my mate's next egg's next egg's next egg,
stegosaur. It's feathers I need, more feathers
for the life to come…
I will teach my sons and daughters to live
on mist and fire and fly to the stars.

—EDWIN MORGAN, *THE ARCHAEOPTERYX'S SONG*

The most thoroughly studied wild bird in the world may be the Great Tit, a bird found across the whole of temperate Eurasia, from Ireland to Borneo.

Once, the god Pan had no music. Then (so runs the tale) he fell in love with a water nymph, who rejected him and fled his advances. As he pursued her, she prayed to the other gods to save her honor. In answer to her prayer, they changed her into a stand of water reeds. Thwarted and heartbroken, Pan cut stems from the reeds and fashioned the first panpipe. Driven by the god's breath, music flowed from what was once her body. Her name—and the Greek word for panpipe—was Syrinx.

Deep in the breast of a bird, at the point where the *trachea*, or windpipe, divides to send its passages to the lungs, is a box of cartilage, membrane, and muscle. It, too, is called a *syrinx*. It is the source of a bird's voice, whether that be the squawk of a hen or the outpouring of a nightingale. The syrinx is of ancient lineage—that most unbirdlike cousin of birds, the alligator, has something like one. In most groups of birds, the membranes of the syrinx are controlled by a single pair of muscles. In songbirds, they are manipulated by up to eight pairs. The complexity of the sounds those muscle-driven membranes produce single out the songbirds from the rest of the avian world (except, as you might expect, for those most talkative of non-

songbirds, the parrots, who have extra syrinx muscles, too). The syrinx allows the songbirds to sing.

Ornithologists group songbirds in the order Passeriformes—the passerines, or perching birds. If you really want to know why, you can check out the latest thorough reclassification of the birds of the world, by Charles Sibley and Jon Ahlquist, and wade through a long page of highly technical fine print (the reference is on page 576, if you must know). For the rest of us, who probably don't want to deal with such terms as *aegigognathous*, *tensor propatagialis brevis*, and *acrosome* any more than we absolutely have to, let's just say that card-carrying members of the Passeriformes have a distinctive palate, wing, and foot structure. Their hind toes are long and flexible. They point backward, so a songbird can get a firm, all-around grip on its perch (yes, yes, parrots can do this, too, but their feet are very different). Male perching birds have sperm cells unlike those of other birds—not a feature your average birder is likely to notice, but important enough to stamp them as unique in a scientist's eyes. The babies some of those sperm cells help produce are hatched out blind and helpless—a very different condition from that of a duckling or a poultry chick.

The "true" songbirds, or *oscines*, differ from the rest of the perching birds—as you might expect—in the details of their complex musical box. An oscine has from five to eight pairs of muscles operating its syrinx. One-fifth of the perching birds—the *suboscines*—have no more than four. The suboscines are, in general, not as good at singing as their better-endowed cousins, but at least some of them make up for it with volume. The Central and South American bellbirds, of the suboscine family Cotingidae, produce some of the most ear-shatteringly loud sounds in the animal kingdom. They may not, strictly speaking, be songbirds, but the suboscines certainly deserve a place in this book.

It isn't just anatomy, though, that makes a songbird a songbird. The suboscines, like most birds, are born (or hatched, if you prefer) with their vocal repertoires hard-wired into their brains. Songbirds, by contrast, have to learn their songs, from parents, neighbors, or even the other sounds they hear as they grow. Before songbirds become musicians, they have to be music students.

Voice and inner workings aside, perching birds—though they certainly vary in such things as bill shape or color pattern—are a fairly homogeneous lot. Except for the lyrebirds of Australia—which you might be forgiven for mistaking for some sort of pheasant, at least until they open their beaks and reveal themselves as among the finest vocalists on earth—you probably would have little trouble picking the passerines out of a bird lineup. They are, by and large, small to medium-sized land birds that perch in trees or bushes, cling to grass tops, scratch for food on bare earth, or hop about on suburban lawns.

No perching bird is really large. The heaviest of them all, the Common Raven, can weigh more than three pounds (1.4 kg). The Thick-billed Raven of the highlands of Ethiopia is probably even bigger, but it seems that no one has ever tried to weigh one. Were it not for the hummingbirds, the songbirds would include the smallest of all birds—and many songbirds are considerably smaller than the largest hummer, the Giant Hummingbird of the Andes. The record for World's Smallest Songbird goes to the Pygmy Tit of the Indonesian island of Java, with the North American Bushtit and a tiny rarity from the Philippines, the Miniature Tit-Babbler—a bird unknown to science until 1962—as runners-up. "Tit," by the way, meant "little animal" in Middle English.

At the pinnacle of avian evolution? The largest of the songbirds, this Common Raven surveys its domain.

Size or strength, though, is no guarantee of success in evolution, and the most remarkable thing about the passerines in general, and the songbirds in particular, has been their astonishing, indeed overwhelming, success. That success does not mean that the perching birds have done everything a bird can do. No passerine swims like a duck, wades like a heron, soars over the ocean like an albatross, or stoops from the sky like a falcon. No other group of birds, though, can come close to the Passeriformes in the numbers game.

Besides the Passeriformes, there are about twenty or thirty other orders of birds, depending on whose system of classification you happen to like. Some of them are pretty exclusive. The

A male Red-capped Manakin, one of the most brilliant of the suboscine songbirds, dances before a female in Soberania National Park, Panama.

order Sphenisciformes, for example, contains nothing but penguins, and the Psittaciformes nothing but parrots. One order, the Struthioniformes, contains only a single living bird, the majestic Ostrich. But the Order Passeriformes, by contrast, sweeps in more than half the birds in the world—almost six thousand species, in fifty or so families.

Why are there so many of them? Like many other fascinating questions about science, this one doesn't really have an answer. The ornithologist John Fitzpatrick has put it this (rather technical) way:

> [S]ome aspects of being small-bodied, large-brained, arboreal, diurnal, largely insectivorous, with high metabolic rate, short generation time and vocally sophisticated appear to have endowed members of the passerine clade with the opportunity or propensity to radiate at a rate faster than that characterizing birds of any other clade.

In other words, the songbirds have an evolutionary and ecological edge over other birds, but we can't really say what has given them that edge. We can only describe the way they are and the way they live, describe their success, and suggest that in some way the one is related to the other.

The Passeriformes have been around for at least thirty million years in the Northern Hemisphere, and perhaps for twenty-five million years before that in the Southern. That may seem like a long time, but, as birds go, perching birds—and especially songbirds—are comparative newcomers.

The earliest known bird—or at least the earliest known animal that pretty much everyone agrees is a bird—lived 140 million years ago, in the Jurassic, the heyday of the dinosaurs. In fact, many scientists believe that *Archaeopteryx*, as this creature is called, actually was a sort of dinosaur. This is not a contradiction in terms. It just means, if you accept this theory, that all the later birds, songbirds included, are dinosaurs, too, or at least dinosaur descendants. Some ornithologists, however, vehemently oppose this notion.

Archaeopteryx looks a lot more like a *Velociraptor* with feathers than, say, a canary. That's what makes it so fascinating. In many ways *Archaeopteryx* is a typical small carnivorous dinosaur, with clawed fingers, a long reptilian tail, and a snoutful of teeth. Its arms, though still ending in clawed fingers, are clearly wings (although how well *Archaeopteryx* could fly is a matter of some disagreement). And there are those beautifully preserved feather imprints showing plumes hardly different from those of a modern flying bird.

After *Archaeopteryx*, bird evolution proceeded by leaps and bounds. Only a few million years later, in what is now China and Spain, there were birds with horny beaks, birds with the deep keels on the breastbone that support the huge wing muscles of almost all modern birds, birds that had replaced the long, dinosaurian tail of *Archaeopteryx* with a stub of bone called the *pygostyle* (or, in less formal language, the "parson's nose"). There was even one bird the size of a sparrow— *Eoalulavis hoyasi*, the first dickey-bird. But there were no songbirds—at least not yet.

For the next seventy million years or so—in fact, for the rest of the Age of Reptiles—there were, apparently, lots of birds, but most of them wouldn't fit into the families listed in a modern field guide. That first flush of bird evolution seems to have been largely given over to groups of

New Zealand wrens
may be survivors of
the earliest wave of
songbird evolution.
The New Zealand
Rock Wren hops
among the boulders
of the alpine slopes of
the South Island.

birds that vanished with their dinosaur cousins. Some were really strange, such as *Hesperornis*, a five-foot (1.5-m) long diving bird that had lost its wings almost entirely, shifted its feet so far back on its body that it may have been unable to stand up on land, but had kept—as a sort of evolutionary souvenir of the days of *Archaeopteryx*—a full set of teeth. Others may have looked more like some sort of modern bird, but the bones in their legs formed in a fashion opposite to that in birds today. They are even called *Enantiornithes*, or "opposite birds."

A birder would have found much more that was familiar by the Oligocene, twenty-seven million years after the dinosaurs vanished. The opposite birds and their toothy cousins were long gone. In their place were most of the modern bird groups: ducks, shorebirds, flamingos, and many more. Birding tours would have been well advised, mind you, to avoid South America, where giant predatory flightless birds, some up to ten feet (3 m) tall, with a great scything beak the size of a horse's head, stalked the landscape. They kept it up for the next thirty million years or so, too, and one of them even ended up living in what is now Florida.

But there were, it seems, still no true songbirds. In the Northern Hemisphere, small birds perching in trees were either relatives of today's woodpeckers or cousins of kingfishers. The woodpecker relatives probably looked like the puffbirds of the New World Tropics; or the honeyguides that lead African hunters to bees' nests; or the barbets, whose maddening, repetitive calls have earned them the name "brain-fever bird" in India. Like puffbirds, honeyguides, barbets, and woodpeckers, they were yoke-toed—two of their toes pointed forward and two back, a quite different arrangement from the three-forward-one-back of songbirds (and most other birds, as well). The kingfisher cousins resembled the gemlike todies of the West Indies—the birds Jamaicans mean when they say "robin redbreast."

In the Southern Hemisphere, the suboscine perching birds had already put in an appearance. But it was the next epoch, the Miocene, that rang in the triumph of the true songbirds, the oscines. By its end the oscines had forced the yoke-toed perchers out of their top spots in the northern forests. In the Old World they pushed the suboscines out of all but the corners of the tropical rainforest, where the brilliant broadbills and pittas survive today, and the island of Madagascar, home of the four species of asities.

Pushed even farther, to the remote land of New Zealand, were the New Zealand wrens. While the oscines have, you will recall, eight pairs of muscles manipulating their syrinx, New Zealand wrens have none at all. They may be suboscines, or all that is left of a line of songbirds that evolved even before the suboscines. Only two species survive today. Two more have disappeared within the past hundred years, including one that was both discovered and exterminated by a lighthouse-keeper's cat.

Only in South America did the suboscines manage to withstand the oscine tide. Almost every "little brown job" in South America is a suboscine, usually an antbird or an ovenbird (not to be confused with the Ovenbird of North America, which is an oscine). So are some of its most brilliant tropical delights, such as the dancing manakins and the cocks-of-the-rock. One suboscine family, the tyrant flycatchers, even reversed the invasion, spreading as far north as Alaska. In much of North

America, the suboscine kingbirds still lord it over their upstart, if more musical, oscine cousins.

Over most of the world, though, the success story of the Passeriformes is really the triumphal march of the oscines. Four out of five perching birds in the world are oscines—more than 4,700 species. If you leave out South America, the odds of any perching bird you meet being an oscine are far higher. All the passerines of Europe, home of the Skylark and the Nightingale, are oscines. Europe is where the word "songbird" was invented. Shakespeare's songbirds—

> *The ousel-cock so black of hue,*
> *With orange-tawny bill,*
> *The throstle with his note so true,*
> *The wren with little quill*

—are all oscines, even if we now call the "ousel-cock" the European Blackbird and the "throstle" the Song Thrush. So are warblers, bluebirds, redstarts, chats, babblers, thrushes, crows, jays, magpies, wagtails, pipits, starlings, sparrows, finches, tanagers, sunbirds, whistlers, flowerpeckers, drongos, swallows, martins, orioles, vireos, waxwings, mockingbirds, thrashers, catbirds, honeyeaters, white-eyes, whipbirds, titmice, and treecreepers. So are akalats, eremomelas, cisticolas, cochoas, akepas, parotias, melampittas, chowchillas, parduscos, cutias, kokakos, and kinkimavos. So are standardwings, barwings, redwings, forktails, wagtails, fantails, emutails, parrotbills, longbills, bristlebills, wedgebills, redthroats, whitethroats, yellowthroats, spotthroats, thickheads, yellowheads, whiteheads, even Bornean Bristleheads. So, indeed, are the birds-of-paradise, once thought to dwell in Heaven itself.

Heaven aside, the oscines have spread from the shores of the Arctic Ocean to the tip of Cape Horn, across the seas to the most distant islands ships can reach, and from the seashore to the heights of the Andes and the high plateaus of Tibet. Of all the continents, only the Antarctic has remained closed to them. The closest they get to it is the windswept island of South Georgia. There, a single species of songbird, the South Georgia Pipit, finds its only home among the

Extreme plumage: A male Wilson's Bird-of-Paradise, of Waigeo and Batanta islands off western New Guinea, fluffs its multi-hued feathers in display.

clumps of tussock grass and the thousands of nesting albatrosses, petrels, and penguins that otherwise make the island a forbidding, but thrilling, place for ornithologists.

There are oscines with such dull plumage and so few visible marks of identification that only an expert armed with a battery of manuals can figure out what they might be, and there are oscines clad in so conflicting a patchwork of brilliant colors that a designer who tried to use

Extreme form: Another New Guinea songbird, the Wattled Ploughbill, combines a thick, strong bill (used to rip open bamboo stems) with, in the male, peculiar fleshy flaps at its gape.

such a scheme would be howled out of the showroom. There are oscines with songs so brilliant and complex that they have inspired whole musical compositions, and others that can barely manage a hoarse squawk. There are oscines so shy and hard to see that they can drive the most experienced and patient birder to despair, and others that will land on your head and try to pull out your hair (should you have any) for nesting material. No, really—a White-eared Honeyeater used to do this to me on a regular basis while I was studying birds in an eastern Australian forest in the early 1970s. It's one of the species' regular habits.

Songbird behavior, in fact, has kept scientists in research material for decades. So many papers have been written about the Great Tits of the woodlands near Oxford University's Edward Grey Institute for Ornithology that they have been jokingly dubbed the laboratory mice of the bird world. Some songbird behaviors display astonishing levels of intricacy, intelligence, or both. Songbirds have relatively large brains, as birds go. A bigger brain—even a relatively bigger brain—doesn't necessarily mean a more intelligent animal, but the oscines at least appear to be extraordinary learners. This may have something to do with learning their complicated songs, but whatever the reason, songbirds have certainly turned their intelligence to other things. The Blue Tit of Europe is famous for having learned to open the foil caps on milk bottles and drink the cream—a habit that spread as other Blue Tits watched, and imitated, their neighbors.

Crows and their cousins aren't outstanding singers, but they are well known for their brain power. Ravens can learn to count to seven. Blue Jays can learn which butterflies are edible by watching jays in the next cage. Captive Blue Tits may have been trained to pull up food suspended on a string, but Northern Ravens, given the same test, were able to figure out how to retrieve the food without training.

In 1970, I discovered that a crow on the remote Pacific island of New Caledonia uses a twig as a tool to probe for insects in hollow branches. Twenty-two years later, a graduate zoology student from New Zealand, Gavin Hunt, returned to New Caledonia for a three-year study of the crows. Hunt discovered that New Caledonian Crows not only use tools, but actually make them. The crows trim and shape twigs and strips of barbed leaf into two types of hooked insect picks, and carry the finished results around with them through the forest—a level of sophistication in tool manufacture and use that Hunt says did not appear even in humans until after the Lower Paleolithic.

Intelligence may help songbirds explore new environments. That may ultimately spawn anatomical change and, perhaps, the evolution of new species. Given our own history, it is

(following page) At the farthest reaches of the oscine advance: The South Georgia Pipit, confined to the island from which it takes its name, is the only songbird to reach the Antarctic.

nice to know that intelligence may actually lead to evolutionary success—at least in birds.

Sophistication, of course, may or may not mean intelligence. People have marveled for centuries at the complexity and beauty of songbird nests—certainly among the most intricate structures in the animal kingdom—and wondered whether instinctive need, intelligent planning, or even a sense of art lay behind their elegant shapes and delicate designs. Why do the penduline tits of Eurasia and Africa take up to twenty-four days to build beautiful little pouches of felt, made from the down of bulrush seeds, animal hairs, and grass fibers, when other birds get by with something much simpler and coarser? Why do male weaverbirds of Africa and Asia vie with one another to build woven purses of grass bound together with real knots and accessible, in some species, only through entrance tubes twice as long as the nest itself?

The most remarkable and puzzling structures songbirds build, though, are not nests. In Australia and New Guinea, male bowerbirds lure females by creating structures so elaborate that, in one case, a scientist mistook them for human artifacts. Bowerbirds don't just build their bowers, but guard them; decorate them with shells, bones, lichen, or flowers; and even paint their walls with the juice of crushed berries. Some ornithologists, bowled over by the apparent genius and sensitivity of these avian architects, have called bowerbirds the pinnacle of bird evolution. That is probably going too far, but any group of animals that can include creatures like the bowerbirds in its ranks is a group worth knowing.

Though we humans may find it hard to accept the fact, brains aren't everything when it comes to succeeding in nature. Surely one of the reasons the passerines have done so well relates, not to their mental agility, but to their physical plasticity. Songbirds have proven themselves to be masters of adaptation, capable of evolutionary shifts and changes that have allowed them to diversify into range after range of surprising types. It is not really odd that a key clue that sent Charles Darwin in pursuit of his theory of evolution by natural selection came from songbirds—or, rather, one particular group of them, the finches of the Galápagos Islands. Even Darwin's finches, though, only begin to show us what songbirds can do.

There may be no songbirds that can swim and dive like loons or grebes. There are, however, the dippers, who plunge into cold mountain torrents and swim, with their wings, along the bottom, heedless of the rushing current as they search for the larvae of caddisflies. There are no songbird falcons, but there are the shrikes, who hunt for mice and smaller birds and impale their carcasses on thorns for safekeeping. In Australia and New Guinea, the melodious butcherbirds do the same thing.

In the New World Tropics the suboscine woodcreepers scale forest trees like woodpeckers, while over much of the rest of the world nuthatches climb down them in ways no woodpecker can match. Woodcreepers and nuthatches don't have the woodpecker's excavating equipment, but in parts of the world that lack woodpeckers there are a few songbirds that do. On the island of Hawaii, a place woodpeckers never reached, lives the Akiapolaau, an endangered

A White-eared Honeyeater gathers nesting material. The gentleman in the photo is not the author, though honeyeaters have found the author useful for the same purpose.

species that may be the world's least finchlike finch. Its bill is a strange-looking mismatch. The upper mandible is long, thin, and curved like a hook, while the lower is stout and straight, like a chisel. The Akiapolaau chips away at wood with its lower mandible, holding the upper out of the way until it uncovers a grub. Then it uses the upper mandible to drag out its prey, spearing it like an olive on a toothpick.

The North Island of New Zealand was once home to an even odder "woodpecker" substitute, the Huia. In the Huia, the division of labor was not between the mandibles but between the sexes. The male Huia had a short, straight beak like a chisel. The female's bill was a true billhook, thin, curved like a scimitar, and much longer than the male's. So different were male and female that they were originally described as separate species.

Pairs of Huias foraged together through the forest in search of their favorite food, the woodboring grub of the *huhu* beetle. In 1864, the New Zealand-born naturalist Sir Walter Lawry Buller obtained a pair of Huias from a Maori hunter. His notes are the best evidence we have for how the Huias used their oddly assorted bills:

> *But what interested me most of all was the manner in which the birds assisted one another in their search for food, because it appeared to explain the use, in the economy of nature, of the differently-formed bills in the two sexes. To divert the birds, I introduced a log of decayed wood infested with the* huhu *grub. They at once attacked it, carefully probing the softer parts with their bills, and then vigorously assailing them, scooping out the decayed wood till the larva or pupa was visible, when it was carefully drawn from its cell, treated in the way described above, and then swallowed. The very different development of the mandibles in the two sexes enabled them to perform separate offices. The male always attacked the more decayed portions of the wood, chiselling out his prey after the manner of some woodpeckers, while the female probed with her long pliant bill the other cells, where hardness of the surrounding parts resisted the chisel of her mate.*

(opposite) **A male Akiapolaau attacks a branch with his unique dual-purpose bill. His lower mandible is a chisel, his upper a hook to spear any grubs his digging may expose. Found only on the island of Hawaii, the Akiapolaau is an endangered species.**

(opposite) **A male of the now-extinct Huia hammers at a limb, while his mate waits below to probe for** *huhu* **grubs with her very different, and much longer, bill. The male's pose is taken from a drawing of a living bird by Walter Buller. Painted by Barry Kent MacKay.**

Alas, we will never know more. By the 1880s, the Huia, pursued by collectors and traders for its strange bill and beautiful black, white-tipped tail feathers, attacked by diseases brought to New Zealand by birds introduced from other lands, and hemmed in to ever-smaller patches of native forest, had already begun to vanish. Sometime after the turn of the century, perhaps as early as 1908, its haunting, flutelike call was heard for the last time.

The fate of the Huia has been shared by many island songbirds, and may soon be shared on the continents by far more. Part of the songbird story is the threat that, thanks to human activities throughout the world, their triumphant evolutionary march may now be grinding to a halt. It is no secret that animals and plants of all kinds are disappearing from the earth, and it ought to be no secret that their disappearance is a warning to our own species. One of the commonest analogies for that warning involves a songbird, the miner's canary, whose death warns of a fate that those carrying it may share if they do not act in self-defense.

We have probably been inspired by them for as long as we have been human. For many birds that inspiration has come from our view of them either as items for the table or as emblems of power. The songbirds, though, have always seemed to me to bring out the better side of human nature, in music, art, poetry, dance, reflection, contemplation, or just the sheer enjoyment of nature for its own sake. Today, we stand, unfortunately, on the brink of losing many of them through our own foolishness, impoverishing our lives in the process. The Huia may serve as a symbol of what there is to lose. The miner's canary should warn us to do something about it before it is too late. Songbirds—in all their brilliance and variety—are worth listening to.

Barry Kent MacKay

NOTICING SONGBIRDS

"You won't like it here," my mother told me. "There aren't any birds. I haven't seen one since I arrived."

The year was 1968, and I had (lucky me) joined my parents in Hong Kong for a vacation. The next morning, I sat happily at my hotel window in downtown Kowloon, watching flocks of chirping Eurasian Tree Sparrows on the pavement below, and rows of fat black Crested Mynas cackling from the telephone wires. My mother—a remarkably intelligent and gifted woman—was, for once, wrong. There were birds everywhere.

Many people have a blind eye for songbirds. When Toronto picked "Blue Jays" as the name for its baseball team, someone indignantly complained to the *Toronto Star* that the choice was entirely unsuitable. Blue Jays, he wrote, didn't exist in Toronto. Of course these spectacular birds—one of the showiest and noisiest in North America—live all over the city. A few days before that complaining letter appeared, I had watched some ten thousand of them heading south, in flock after flock, through Toronto's High Park.

If you are already a birder, you're probably chuckling over these stories (you probably know a few like them yourself). If you aren't, you may be getting frustrated already. Why, you may ask, can some people spot birds all over the place, even tell what they are, when you yourself can't see a thing?

There's no magic to it, of course. Anyone can enjoy songbirds. You don't have to be a bird-watcher to do it—but you do have to become something else: a bird -noticer.

Noticing songbirds is really a part of being aware of nature. There's no trick to watching sparrows on a lawn or starlings on a pavement. Many songbirds, though, don't make themselves obvious. They sit in the crowns of trees or dash into bushes as you pass.

If you want to see them, you have to pay attention to rustling branches and quivering leaves, and hunt for the thing that makes them rustle and quiver.

Most of all, you have to use your ears. After all, we don't call them "songbirds" for nothing. Many songbirds are easier to hear than they are to see. Some, like the North American Connecticut Warbler or the Australian Rufous Scrub-Bird, are so much easier that they remain disembodied voices to all but the most hard-core and persistent of birders. Fortunately, during the breeding season they announce their presence so forcefully, and so distinctively, that anyone who knows bird songs will know not only that they are there, but what they are.

If you really want to appreciate how many songbirds there are around you, you must be about when they are. Birds are most active early in the morning. There is all the difference in the world between a spring forest at dawn, ringing with the different songs of its varied birds, and the same place in the heat of the day, when the only voice is the whine of the cicada.

So, to be a bird-noticer, get out into the woods (or the fields, or the marshes, or whatever you have nearby). Be there when the sun rises, especially in spring, when the birds are breeding and singing. Watch and listen. If you ever thought that birds were hard to find, you should soon change your mind. Once you do, you can move on, not just to naming the birds you see, but to learning about what they do. And while you are looking and listening for birds, you will surely find other things, as well—a toad under a leaf, a beetle scaling a tree, squirrels, flowers, ferns. You will become something far better than a bird-noticer, or even a birder. You will become a naturalist.

A WORLD OF SONGBIRDS

What shulde I sayn? Of foules every kynde
That in this world han fethers and stature
Man myghten in that place assembled fynde
Byfore the noble goddesse Nature…

—GEOFFREY CHAUCER, *THE PARLIAMENT OF FOWLS*

Few birds are as spectacular as a male Guianan Cock-of-the-Rock, a cotinga from northeastern South America. In display, he spreads his crest forward, covering his bill.

Songbirds impress us, not with their size or strength or grandeur, but with their sheer variety. That variety has been achieved, over and over again, through a series of evolutionary radiations, as songbirds expanded their numbers and range on continent after continent, filling the vacant niches in each new environment. This chapter follows these radiations, looking at the assortment of birds that each has produced.

It has taken us a long time to appreciate not just the variety of songbirds, but their ability to vary. Before Darwin, variability wasn't an issue—the potential to create variety was not the birds' but God's. Even after evolution became the defining concept of biology, most ornithologists placed thin-billed, wrenlike insect eaters in one family; broad-billed, sallying flycatchers in another; and thick-billed, seed-cracking finches in still another. Their assumption seemed to be that each type evolved only once or twice and, having arisen, simply produced minor variations as it spread around the globe.

While Old World warblers are clad mostly in shades of olive green and brown, North Americans are treated each spring to a riot of flickering colors as migrating wood warblers

scatter through the growing leaves, fluttering like the butterflies their brilliance recalls. Many nineteenth-century ornithologists greeted with disbelief the notion, first suggested (before Darwin!) in 1838, that the American wood warblers not only were unrelated to their European counterparts, but were each other's closest cousins. As late as 1885, the eminent British scientist R. Bowdler Sharpe was still insisting that some were wrens, others fly-catchers, and the largest of the lot, the Yellow-breasted Chat, a vireo. The chat, in fact, did not earn its permanent place among the warblers until comparatively recently. A peculiar long-legged, short-tailed little bird from Central America, the Wrenthrush, recently turned out to be a warbler, too.

The old assumption was wrong. Warblerlike songbirds, flycatcherlike songbirds, finchlike songbirds did not evolve once, but over and over again, as each new land filled with oscine invaders. In the course of these repeated cycles of invasion and radiation, songbirds from quite different families came to resemble one another. Thus, the Western Meadowlark of America's prairies parallels the unrelated Yellow-throated Longclaw of the African veldt. They are not related, but *convergent.* They look, and act, alike because both, by living in similar habitats, have faced similar evolutionary pressures.

Ornithologists have searched everything from behavior and anatomy to biochemistry for clues telling us how birds are related to one another. The most recent attempt to trace the pattern of songbird evolution—by Charles Sibley and Jon Ahlquist—is based on a chemical technique called DNA-DNA hybridization. The technique, basically, involves "unzipping" the DNA strands and seeing how well single strands from one species pair up with single strands from another. The more similar the genes of the two species are, the better the fit should be. Closeness of fit is, therefore, a measure of how recently the two birds have shared an identical common ancestor, and that in turn shows how closely they are related to each other.

The arrangement Sibley and Ahlquist derived from their DNA results has upset many of our traditional ideas about bird relationships. It has yet to be accepted as the basis for classifying birds in field guides and natural histories. It does, however, give us an excellent framework for examining the evolution of songbirds. Though we will not worry here about the precise details of which family is which, the songbird family tree according to DNA-DNA hybridization will be our guide through much of this chapter.

Of the earliest songbird radiation only a vestige may remain, a vestige that has grown even smaller during the past hundred years. It shrank in 1894, when the lighthouse-keeper's cat on Stephens Island, a rock off the coast of New Zealand, brought a handful of tiny feathered corpses to his master's stoop. They were all that was left of the Stephens Island Rock Wren, a bird unknown to science until that time and never seen alive again. The Stephens Island Wren was one of four surviving New Zealand wrens, perhaps the most primitive of living passerine birds. A second species, the Bush Wren, disappeared in the 1960s. Fortunately, the two species that remain, the Rock Wren of the alpine slopes on the South Island and the Rifleman, a tiny, gregarious forest bird something like a cross between a warbler and a nuthatch, seem reasonably secure.

(opposite) Similar patterns, dissimilar origins: Though the Western Meadowlark of North America (left) and the Yellow-throated Longclaw of Africa (right) resemble each other, they belong to different songbird families. The meadowlark is related to American orioles and blackbirds, the longclaw to wagtails and pipits. Their resemblance is an example of convergent evolution.

A Rufous Hornero, one of the South American ovenbirds, stands in its half-completed nest. When finished, its sphere of sun-baked clay may last for years.

The greatest suboscine radiation produced the dominant songbirds of the tropical forests of the New World: ovenbirds, antbirds, woodcreepers, gnateaters, cotingas, manakins, tapaculos, and tyrant flycatchers. Most do not leave the Tropics, but the ovenbirds have penetrated southward to Patagonia and the tyrant flycatchers are well represented in North America.

We northerners may dismiss the ovenbirds, or confuse them with the wood warbler that carries that name. But the Furnariidae, the ovenbird family, is one of the largest, most diverse, and—though furnariids lack the garish colors of more famous South American birds—most fascinating groups of birds on earth.

More than two hundred species of ovenbirds live in rainforests, dry woodlands, alpine screes, and the windswept plains of Patagonia. They run the gamut of passerine lifestyles. There are ovenbird equivalents to jays, thrashers, tits, nuthatches, and—especially if we include their close cousins the woodcreepers—woodpeckers. A few variations of their own have been given evocative English names to match, though these mean little to the people who live among them: earthcreeper, treehunter, foliage-gleaner, leaftosser, Firewood-Gatherer, miner. In the marshlands of the pampas, the Wrenlike Rushbird and the Curve-billed Reedhaunter are near dead ringers for, respectively, a North American Marsh Wren and a European Great Reed Warbler.

Ovenbird nests range from the burrows of miners, earthcreepers, and leaftossers through an array of unique and complicated structures. Some rainforest ovenbirds build thick, roofed nests of moss. The six horneros build round clay "ovens," the nests that give the family its name, with a coiling inner passage like the interior of a snail shell to make it harder for predators to enter. Ovens of the Rufous Hornero, Argentina's national bird, are a familiar sight on fence posts and telephone poles in Argentina, Uruguay, and southern Brazil. Alexander Skutch, an ornithologist who has spent much of his long life in the New World Tropics, has

written that ovenbird nests are "often so much larger than their small builders that they might be called the birds' castles, and the family to which they belong, castlebuilders." In the southern Brazilian state of Rio Grande do Sul, Firewood-Gatherers have caused short-circuits and fires by raising their castles of sticks atop electrical installations, their bulwarks laced with bits of metal wire.

The 250 or so species of antbird are mostly confined to tropical humid forests and dense thickets. Hard to see, they are certainly easy to hear, or, for some, impossible not to hear, as they repeat their loud churrs, rattles, or whistles. They lack bright feathers, though some sport patches of bare skin, red or bright blue, around their eyes or on their crowns, and the White-plumed Antbird wears a long, stiff tuft of feathers on its forehead and a short white

Antbird plumage is usually somber, but the sparkling white facial plumes of the White-plumed Antbird are an exception.

beard to match. The antthrushes, stolid, almost rectangular birds that stalk like rails over the forest floor, and their thickset, long-legged relatives, the antpittas, may not be as closely related to the other antbirds as we once thought—or, at least, that is what the DNA evidence seems to suggest.

The tapaculos are strange, shy, mouselike birds that creep about on the forest floor from Costa Rica to Tierra del Fuego, whistling, chortling, or trilling like toads. Far more obvious are the tyrant flycatchers, by far the most successful of the suboscines. They alone have carried the suboscine banner north of the Mexican border, where kingbirds, pewees, phoebes, and a range of other species reach as far north as Alaska and as far east as Newfoundland.

Birders in North America picture tyrant flycatchers sitting upright on a perch, or sallying to snatch flying insects. That description fits most flycatchers living north of the Rio Grande. In South America, though, there are flycatchers that look and act like thrushes, shrikes, wagtails, or wheatears; pipitlike flycatchers running about on the bare soil of Patagonia; and titlike flycatchers exploring the branches of moss-laden trees in the high Andes.

Most tyrant flycatchers are not brightly colored, though the Many-colored Rush-Tyrant, a bird of the marshes of southern South America, earns its name—and its Spanish name, *siete colores*, or seven colors—with a patchwork plumage of red, orange, blue, green, yellow, black, and white. Some, like the Scissor-tailed Flycatcher and the Streamer-tailed Tyrant, sport elongated tail plumes. Southeastern South America is home to two extraordinary creatures: the increasingly rare Strange-tailed Tyrant, named for its long, twisting outer tail feathers ending in black flags, and the even odder Cock-tailed Tyrant, whose wide, stiffened central tail feathers stick up like the plumes of a bantam rooster, giving its tail a three-bladed silhouette like the back end of an airplane.

Though insect eaters, most tyrant flycatchers will take fruit if they can get it. Their close relatives the manakins and cotingas are fruit specialists. Their colorful plumage, startling displays, and sprightly dances make manakins and cotingas suboscine rivals of the Old World birds-of-paradise. The compact, brilliant manakins concentrate on small fruits on shrubs and lower trees.

Male Asian Paradise-Flycatchers may be brown or white. A white male, like this one, is one of the most ethereal-looking of birds.

Cotingas—a group that includes fruitcrows, plantcutters, pihas, umbrellabirds, bellbirds, and cocks-of-the-rock—may be very large birds indeed, feed mostly on larger fruits, and tend to spend more of their time in the forest canopy.

Few birds are as garishly feathered as the male Guianan Cock-of-the-Rock. It isn't just that he is mostly bright orange. A lacy stiff crest on his head may practically hide his bill from sight, while long silky ornamental plumes on his flight feathers, tipped with elaborate lacy fringes, make the entire bird look like a Day-Glo lace doily, especially when he spreads them in display. The Jivaro Indians copy the dance of the other species, the Andean Cock-of-the-Rock, for their own ceremonies.

Umbrellabirds sport a feather parasol dangling over their beaks and a wattle hanging from their chests. In two of the species, the wattle—like the rest of the bird—is covered with black feathers, but in the third, the Bare-necked Umbrellabird, it is nearly featherless and bright red. When the male displays, the whole thing blows up like a great scarlet balloon. That isn't just for looks. Inflating the wattle helps the male make a low-pitched booming call, said to resemble the challenge of a bull.

Bellbirds may be the loudest birds in the world. They have nothing to do with the birds called bellbirds in Australia and New Zealand, which are oscines belonging to the honeyeater family. A male bellbird's *bock*, given from a special "visiting perch" high in a tree, sounds like a sledgehammer striking an anvil. It can be heard up to half a mile (1 km) away. A Bare-throated Bellbird in the London Zoo once *bock*ed at me from about four feet (1 m); my head rang for some time. According to cotinga expert David Snow, when a visitor lands on the perch of a male Three-wattled Bellbird

> *the owning male changes places with it during the display, and then hops up to the visitor and utters close into its ear the changing-place call followed by an extremely loud* bock. *Normally this causes a male visitor to fall or fly off the end of the visiting perch…*

though, Snow notes, it often comes back for more.

The Old World suboscines—the pittas, broadbills, and asities—are more closely related to one another than to the American suboscines. They include some of the most beautiful birds in the world. Pittas were once called "jewel thrushes," and they well deserved it. Chunky, long-legged, short-tailed birds of forest floors from Africa to the Solomons, they are shaped like the New World antpittas that take their name. Unlike them, they are clad in black, white, red, green, yellow, azure blue, glowing orange, or almost anything else (yes, even brown), sometimes in startling arrangements.

The Blue-banded Pitta of Borneo has an orange-red head and scarlet underparts set off by azure bands across the chest and behind the eye. The Superb Pitta of Manus Island, in the

A male Three-wattled Bellbird calls from his display perch in the cloud forests of Costa Rica. His voice may carry for half a mile (1 km).

Admiralties, highlights a glossy black body with broad, iridescent turquoise wing shoulders and a bright-red belly. The male of Thailand's critically endangered Gurney's Pitta has a brown back, black face and belly, white throat, ultramarine-blue crown and tail, and a rich yellow band across his chest and down each flank. Despite such gaudiness, pittas are far easier to hear than to see. The Noisy Pitta of eastern Australia earns its name with a loud, easily imitated *walk-to-work* (or, if you prefer, *hhWup-hu-hWip*) that may begin sounding as early as 3 A.M.

The chunky, big-headed broadbills are—except for three brown, streaky, flycatcherlike birds in Africa—as striking, and often as colorful, as the pittas. They are usually rather inactive, often sitting quietly for long periods in forest trees. In the breeding season, African Broadbills display by jumping into the air from a perch and flying in a tight, horizontal circle or ellipse, accompanied by a peculiar rattling whistle like a recoiling spring, apparently made by vibrations of its stiff, twisted outer wing feathers. The asities (pronounced *a-zee´-tees*) of Madagascar, once placed in their own family, are now known to be broadbills—though the two sunbird-asities belie the family name with a long, narrow, strongly curved bill so like that of the true oscine sunbirds that the Common Sunbird-Asity, the first to be discovered by scientists, went unrecognized as a suboscine for seventy-five years.

For many years, lyrebirds and their close, but far less spectacular, Australian relatives, the scrub-birds, were considered to be suboscines because their syrinx musculature is somewhat simpler than in typical songbirds. More recent studies, however, suggest that they are true oscines after all.

With the lyrebirds and scrub-birds, in fact, we come to one of the two great oscine radiations, the last to be recognized for what it truly was. Only with the study of their DNA did we get confirming evidence (though some had suspected it long before) that most of the oscines of Australia—262 out of 302 breeding species—are, despite their apparent similarity to the thrushes, wrens, babblers, warblers, treecreepers, and flycatchers of northern regions, really most closely related to one another. Like the marsupials among the mammals, Australia's

A Red-bellied Pitta, one of the colorful "jewel thrushes" of the Old World Tropics. It lives in the rainforest floor in New Guinea and extreme northern Australia.

A male Superb Lyrebird, hidden beneath the curtain of his fully opened tail, dances on his display ground in south-eastern Australia.

songbirds, isolated on their island continent, have evolved a wide range of body forms, and taken up lifestyles adopted by many different families elsewhere.

The DNA evidence puts the lyrebirds and scrub-birds closest to the bowerbirds and Australian treecreepers, on one of three main sub-branches of the Australian oscine limb of the songbird family tree. Lyrebirds are almost flightless, able to use their wings only for balance or for short downhill glides. Despite their underendowed syrinx, they are probably the most outstanding mimics, and certainly among the most accomplished singers, among birds.

The male Superb Lyrebird is a spectacular creature, more than three feet (1 m) long, half of that taken up by his splendid and peculiar tail. Two outer feathers, gracefully curved, silvery white with chestnut bands—the frame of the lyre—bracket twelve long, lacy filaments and two central streamers like silvered wires. It may take a young lyrebird seven or eight years to develop this ornament. Despite drawings that ended up on early Australian postage stamps, lyrebirds do not hold their tails in a lyre shape. Instead, the male spreads his tail like a fan and bends it forward over his head, where it shakes and shimmers as he dances and sings. Sir Robert Helpmann choreographed a ballet, *The Display*, based on this performance.

Males spend about four months of the year calling for mates on their dancing grounds, cleared and scratched areas of soil about a yard or two (1–2 m) in width. They do nothing to help the female raise her single young. Albert's Lyrebird, the second species—confined to a small area of east-central Australian forest north of the range of its better-known cousin—dances on a tangle of vines, shaking them so that the forest for several yards around joins in his dance.

I chased Australian treecreepers for two years in pursuit of my doctorate. They gave me a chance to see Australia, so I have a very soft spot for these peculiar birds. Not that they are particularly striking—a Brown Treecreeper looks vaguely like a scaled-down immature European Starling, incongruously hitching itself up the side of a eucalyptus trunk. They do have some anatomical peculiarities all their own, including a strengthened, almost columnar hind toe that braces them on their vertical wanderings.

The second sub-branch of the Australian oscine limb centers around one of the most aggressive, successful, and widespread Australasian bird groups—the honeyeater family, Meliphagidae. Not only are there a lot of them—182 species in 42 genera—but honeyeaters have spread throughout Australia and New Guinea, and beyond to the edges of the Australasian region in New Zealand and Hawaii. One species reaches Lombok, the last island a traveler passes before sailing from Australasia over Wallace's Line, the invisible divide between two great biological

Unique if unspectacular: A Brown Treecreeper, one of the distinctive Australian treecreepers. Unlike the unrelated Northern Hemisphere treecreepers, Australian treecreepers do not use their tails as supports when climbing, relying instead on their straight, heavily clawed hind toes.

The tiny Mallee Emu-Wren of southern Australia gets its name from its peculiar tail feathers, which recall the quills of Australia's largest bird, the Emu.

realms, into Tropical Asia. Honeyeaters are one of the most varied of bird families—remarkably so, considering that many of them eat the same foods, nectar and pollen, lapping them up with a long, brush-tipped tongue. They range from the chickadee-sized myzomelas (3 in./8 cm) to the jay-sized friarbirds and jaylike miners.

One of the largest of the family, the thirteen-inch (33-cm) Kioea, was the victim of one of the first historical extinctions on Hawaii. It has not been seen since 1859. The other four Hawaiian honeyeaters, the oos (pronounced *oh-ohs*), graceful, long-tailed blackish birds decorated with tufts of yellow feathers once prized for the royal robes of Hawaiian kings, have fared little better. The Oahu Oo was last collected in 1837, the Hawaii Oo has gone unheard since 1934, and the last of the Kauai Oos seems to have finally disappeared from its only known stronghold, the Alakai Wilderness Preserve in the Kauai highlands. Only Bishop's Oo might just survive in the dense forests on the northeast face of Mount Haleakala, Maui, where a lone bird was seen in 1981.

Related to the honeyeaters are the gemlike fairy-wrens and their cousins the grasswrens and emu-wrens. Emu-wrens are well named. Their long, stiff, disintegrated tail feathers make them look as though someone had plucked an emu and stuffed the results into a creature several sizes too small to carry them. Related, as well, are a host of small warblerlike birds: scrubwrens, thornbills, weebills, whitefaces, gerygones, and pardalotes. The pudgy, colorful little Spotted Pardalote nests in a burrow in the ground but plucks scale insects high in the trees, singing a monotonous, two-note *tank-tink*, a high-pitched "two bits" without the "shave-and-a-haircut."

The third sub-branch of the Australian songbird limb exploded out of Australasia to conquer the rest of the world. Within Australasia, it claims in membership the beautiful and charming Australian "robins." Few birds are lovelier than the Rose Robin, its gray-and-white feathering set off by a soft-pink breast, and few are tamer than the New Zealand Robin, a bird that will stop you on a forest trail to peck at your shoelaces. Its other Australian members are diverse in the extreme: Australian "babblers"; the spiky-tailed logrunners; quailthrushes; whipbirds; the strange, crested, parrot-billed Shriketit that tears eucalyptus bark from its tree in strips as it hunts; sittellas like miniature nuthatches; whistlers; apostlebirds; even the birds-of-paradise. It includes the Pied Butcherbird, one of the world's finest singers, and its relatives the other butcherbirds and Australian Magpies, memorable musicians, too. Not everyone would say the same for their close relative, the large, aggressive, crowlike Pied Currawong, whose raucous *currawong! kraa-ha!* became my daily alarm clock in suburban Sydney.

But the group that gives the whole Australasian assemblage its technical name, the Corvida, has flown far beyond Australia. "Corvida" derives from *Corvus*, the crow. There are crows on every continent but South America (which has jays, instead) and Antarctica (which has no songbirds at all). Crows, ravens, jays, magpies, choughs, and nutcrackers have imposed themselves on our culture. The Common Raven's intelligence, boldness, and resourcefulness have fixed it in our canon of overpowering natural symbols, from the great creative spirit of the Haida, to the guardians who must never leave the Tower of London lest it fall, to the black oracle croaking the fatal entrance of Duncan under Macbeth's battlements or repeating its implacable "nevermore" from atop the pallid bust of Pallas in Poe's *The Raven*. The thieving habits of the Black-billed Magpie have even landed it the title role in an opera, Rossini's *La Gazza ladra*.

The aerobatic woodswallows and the delightful fantails have spread from Australia to Asia. Cuckoo-shrikes, drongos, and monarch flycatchers have gone on to Africa and Asia, where the paradise-flycatchers trail tail streamers sometimes twice their body length that flicker like ribbons in a breeze as they fly. The orioles—the original bearers of that name, no relation to the American birds—even reach Europe. Other members of the Australasian clan abroad do not live in Australia at all, though the shrikes have, in a way, gone home again—one widespread Asian species, the Long-tailed Shrike, is common in open country in New Guinea.

Though members of the Australasian songbird radiation, vireos are found only in the New World. The Black-capped Vireo breeds in Texas and Oklahoma and winters in Mexico. It is one of the rarer members of the family.

One "Australasian" bird family is actually confined to the New World, a hemisphere it may have reached millennia ago via a still-green Antarctic. These are the vireos, with their tropical relations the greenlets, peppershrikes, and shrikevireos. *Vireo* means "I am green," and so most of them are. Green is the predominant color on almost every member of the family, except for a few such as the Golden and Slaty Vireos of Mexico. The Red-eyed Vireo is one of the commonest forest birds in North America. The Black-capped Vireo, breeding only in Texas and Oklahoma, is one of the rarest.

The other great limb of the oscine family tree, the Passerida, the counterpart, or "sister-group," to the Corvida, probably arose in Africa or Eurasia. As the dominant songbirds of England, they were the first to bear the names sparrow, robin, wren, blackbird, thrush, warbler, flycatcher, creeper, and tit, before travelers and colonists applied them to birds both related and unrelated the world over.

There are two main branches of the Passerida. One includes waxwings, dippers, bulbuls, tits, nuthatches, and the surprisingly closely related starlings of the Old World and mockingbirds of the New. Its chief members, though, are a huge host of largely Old World insect-eating birds.

The European naturalists' clear idea of what a warbler was, or a flycatcher, or a thrush, collapsed when they began to explore the Tropics. Here were warblerlike thrushes, flycatcherlike warblers, thrushlike flycatchers, and babblers (whose only apparent European representative, the Bearded Reedling, was mistaken for a tit) that looked like all three. One obscure creature from the island of Príncipe in West Africa, *Horizorhinus dohrni*, is so impossible to classify that a friend of mine, in frustration, christened it the thrush-warbler-flycatcher-babbler. Less picky ornithologists call it Dohrn's Flycatcher. To add to the confusion, DNA results suggested that many of the thrushes *were* actually flycatchers; that the "warblers" in the genus *Sylvia* that gave the Old World warbler "family" its traditional name, Sylviidae, were actually babblers; and that some of the birds usually tossed into this vast pot belonged to other songbird families altogether. The supposed "Old World warblers" in the New World turn out either to be wrens (the gnatcatchers and their kin) or off in a family of their own (the kinglets).

Perhaps we should just say here that there are a great many of these birds and they are all (or nearly all) related to one another in some way, and leave it at that, though with a word for the most glorious band of avian songsters, the thrushes, who sing from Tierra del Fuego around the world to the farthest reaches of the Pacific.

Truly distinctive within this branch of the Passerida are the swallows. Beautifully adapted for life on the wing, swallows have spread the world over without varying their elegant body plan very much. The Barn Swallow is, except for those species we have transplanted ourselves, the most widely occurring songbird in the world. It breeds on five continents and shows up fairly regularly on a sixth, Australia, where a closely related swallow lives instead. Strangest of the swallows are the two river martins, one in the Congo basin and a rare species far away in Thailand. African River Martins indulge in evening flights of thousands of birds that gather in a twisting, pulsing mass like a single, amorphous living thing.

The second branch of the Passerida includes the larks, sunbirds, flowerpeckers, sparrows, pipits, weavers and weaver- or grass-finches, and the "true" finches. One of its stocks, though—a stock with only nine fully developed primary flight feathers, instead of the usual ten—reached the New World, where it radiated again to produce an array of "nine-primaried oscines." In the Old World, the nine-primaried group is represented only by the buntings. In the New, it includes the American sparrows (which are really buntings, quite unlike the House Sparrow and its relatives from the Old World), the cardinals, American grosbeaks, tanagers, honeycreepers, Bananaquit, and wood warblers—themselves so variable that, as we have seen, nineteenth-century naturalists could not fit them comfortably within a single family. The New World nine-primaried group also includes the American blackbirds, which themselves include birds as diverse as grackles, cowbirds, meadowlarks, Bobolinks, American orioles, caciques, and the huge colonial oropendolas.

The great continental songbird radiations have been mirrored, in miniature, whenever songbirds have flown, or have been driven, out over the sea to islands. An oceanic island—one that has never been part of a continent—arises from the waters free of life, an empty slate for nature to

The most widespread songbird in the world is the **Barn Swallow,** a bird that nests in barns and under eaves on every continent but **Australia** and **Antarctica.**

write upon. A songbird landing on the barren rocks of a new island is almost surely doomed, but give that island time to collect seeds, grow plants, fill with windblown insects and spiders, and birds that land there may find not just a new home but a host of new evolutionary opportunities. Freed from the constraints of continental life, where the ecological vacancies are already filled, its descendants may evolve into shapes and forms so distinct that their ancestry itself is blurred.

There is no better example of this than the Hawaiian Islands, at least formerly the most remote archipelago on earth. Before a wave of extinctions wiped many of them out, Hawaii was home to one of the most fascinating assemblages of birds on the planet. The Hawaiian honeycreepers differ from one another so much that if Darwin had visited Hawaii instead of the Galápagos, evolution might never have occurred to him. Who could imagine that the massivebilled Kona Grosbeak cracking hard, dry *naio* fruits on the lava slopes was close cousin to the Akialoa tapping bark crevices with its long, slender, down-curved beak? Or to the black-and-yellow, scythe-billed Mamo probing for nectar in the flowers of lobelias? Or to the little, stubbilled Ula-ai-hawane, clad in red, black, and frosted gray, of whose life we, alas, know nothing?

Yet all these birds—every one of them now extinct—were the products of a single radiation, (this page) **Evolution in action: The Medium Ground-Finch of the Galápagos Islands. The upper bird is a small-billed, black male from Santa Cruz. The larger-billed birds at the bottom are from San Cristobal. The bird at left is a female. The male on her right is not yet in adult plumage—a plumage some males never attain. Painted by Barry Kent Mackay.**

(opposite page) **An extreme island radiation: Three vangas from Madagascar—the Helmet Vanga of the northeastern rain-forests (top), the Sickle-billed Vanga of the dry west (middle), and the widespread Blue Vanga (bottom). Painted by Barry Kent Mackay.**

whose ancestor was once thought to be a thin-billed honeycreeper from the New World but was almost certainly a finch, perhaps something like a redpoll, probably from the Old. Fortunately, not all the Hawaiian honeycreepers (or Hawaiian finches, as some now call them) are gone. The weirdest of the lot, the Akiapolaau, which we met in Chapter One, still survives. So, I am glad to say, does one of my favorite birds, the Iiwi. Try to imagine a pint-sized Scarlet Tanager lookalike with a voice like a squeaky hinge, an immense salmon-colored sickle of a bill, the acrobatic talents of a chickadee, and an attitude.

People don't often notice it because they're too busy getting excited about their brilliant colors and wonderful displays, but New Guinea's birds-of-paradise provide another island example of adaptive radiation in feeding type, their bills ranging from the short, sturdy beak of the King Bird-of-Paradise to the long, narrow probe of the sicklebills. So do the Vangas of Madagascar, whose beaks have been compared to an array of surgical instruments. So, of course, do the most famous of them all, the Galápagos finches.

The most interesting thing about the Galápagos finches is, paradoxically, that they haven't radiated very much. Except for the insect-eating Warbler Finch, the different species are still quite similar to one another. Nobody could possibly confuse an Iiwi with a Palila, or a Sickle-billed Vanga with a Nuthatch Vanga, but telling a Medium Ground-Finch from a Large Ground-Finch can be a genuine puzzler. The Galápagos finches are a radiation that is just starting to happen, one that lets us watch evolution in the act.

Charles Darwin did not get his ideas about evolution from watching the Galápagos finches (he didn't even realize they were all finches, or that they were confined to the Galápagos). The possibilities that they present did not strike him in full until much later. On the *Beagle*, he did not even label his specimens by island until he neared the end of his stay. The most valuable and intensive study of the evolution of the Galápagos finches was conducted not by Darwin, but by Peter and Rosemary Grant and their students in our own time. The Grants have concentrated for more than twenty years on a single population of Medium Ground-Finches on the small island of Daphne Major. What they have recorded there is nothing less than evolution in action.

Ground-finch bills vary somewhat in thickness from bird to bird. While the Grants were studying the island, a severe drought eliminated most of the plants that produce small and easy-to-open seeds. Ground-finches with larger bills were better able to survive under these conditions, and in the space of a few generations the average beak size of the finches on Daphne had increased significantly. When the rains returned, the restraints on the survival of smaller-billed individuals were lifted and the averages shifted back the other way. It does not take much imagination or deductive reasoning to understand that if conditions really change for good, the change in the finches might become permanent, too. If anyone ever tells you that the evolution that has produced our multivaried world of songbirds is just a theory, that nobody has ever seen it happen, please refer him, or her, to the finches of Daphne Major.

GETTING THE NAMES STRAIGHT

Why was the Baltimore Oriole called "Northern Oriole" for a while, but is now back to "Baltimore Oriole" again? It is bad enough having to remember them all—but why do bird names keep changing? And if the English names weren't bad enough, there are all those Latin names… There are few things more confusing for a beginning birder—or for many an experienced one—than naming the birds.

Latin, or scientific, names are perhaps easier to explain. The scientific system for naming living things goes back to the Swedish botanist Karl von Linné, known in Latin as Linnaeus, and the third edition of his book *Systema Naturae*, published in 1758. Linnaeus' system gives each species a double, or *binomial*, name—*Icterus galbula* for the Baltimore Oriole, for instance. Think of this as being like a person's name, with the last name first. The second word, *galbula*, is the bird's "given name" or *specific epithet*—it belongs only to the Baltimore. The first word, *Icterus*, tells us that the Baltimore Oriole belongs in a larger group, or *genus*, which includes other orioles, such as the Orchard Oriole, *Icterus spurius*, or Scott's Oriole, *Icterus parisorum*.

Scientific names are coined according to a series of strict rules called the International Code of Zoological Nomenclature. Nomenclaturists have drawn heavily on history and the classics in coming up with them, producing a world in which Attila and his brother Bleda are not conquering Huns, but a tyrant flycatcher and a bulbul, respectively. *Icterus*, though, simply means (in Greek) a yellow bird. So does *galbula*, this time in Latin.

The Code also contains rules for changing names if necessary. Ornithologists studying a bird may decide that it belongs in a different genus (so the generic name changes), or that it should be "lumped" as part of another species (so the specific epithet changes). For a while, the Baltimore Oriole was "lumped" with its western counterpart, Bullock's Oriole, *Icterus bullockii*. Both were called by the older name, *Icterus galbula*. Since English names (at least as we use them today) are supposed to apply to a whole species, not just part of it, a new English name had to be found that fitted both birds—hence "Northern Oriole." However, we now believe that both birds should in fact be treated as separate species—so we are back to Baltimore and Bullock's again.

This kind of change, the opposite of a *lump*, is called a *split*. Other splits have recently changed the Brown Towhee into the California and Canyon Towhees, and separated the Black-tailed Gnatcatchers of the California chaparral from other Black-tails as the California Gnatcatcher—creating a storm of controversy in the process, because the California Gnatcatcher is (a) a Threatened Species under U.S. law, and (b) lives on land coveted by developers.

This is by no means as haphazard and arbitrary as it sounds. Name changes reflect, or should reflect, changes in our knowledge. That goes for the "official" English names, too, which are supposed to track the changes in scientific names, though sometimes a name will change to match that used for the same bird in another part of the world (for example, the Gray-headed Chickadee of Alaska is called "Siberian Tit" in Europe). Official names, both scientific and English, are decided in North America by a group of professional ornithologists, the Checklist Committee of the American Ornithologists' Union.

The oriole name changes reflect our ideas about what a species is. The "classical" definition of a species is a population of animals (or plants) whose members do not interbreed with members of other populations. In North America, many species were probably divided into eastern and western representatives by tongues of ice from the last glaciation. In isolation, each population developed enough differences so that when the ice disappeared and the birds encountered their relatives again, they did not interbreed. The eastern Baltimore and western Bullock's Orioles, though, do interbreed where they meet. Nature is rarely neat. Even if two forms of birds interbreed, their hybrids may be sterile, like mules. Almost all hybrids between Eastern and Western Meadowlarks are sterile—or simply do so poorly that you can find them only in a very narrow zone, where they may survive because neither of their parent forms is in first-class habitat. That proved to be the case with the orioles, and we now think that their limited interbreeding is not enough to justify lumping them.

If names do not stand still, neither does nature. In eastern North America, interbreeding between Blue-winged and Golden-winged Warblers produces hybrids distinctive enough to be illustrated in most bird guides. This has been going on only since settlers cleared most of the eastern forest in the mid-1800s. That allowed the two species, which prefer edge and scrub, to meet and interbreed. The Blue-winged usually replaces the Golden-winged within fifty years. As it moves north, the Golden-winged may slowly, but inevitably, disappear.

AVIAN IMPERATIVES

Thus when the swallow, seeking prey,
Within the sash is closely pent,
His consort, with bemoaning lay,
Without, sits pining for the event.
Her chattering lovers all around her skim;
She heeds them not (poor bird)—her soul's with him.

—JOHN GAY, *THE BEGGAR'S OPERA*

In southeastern Australia, the New Holland Honeyeater defends a larger territory when banksias, like this one, are in flower than it does when the more nectar-rich grevilleas bloom.

Songbirds, like any other animal, have two basic purposes in life: to survive and to reproduce. In the evolutionary sweepstakes only the reproduction really counts. The sole way for a living thing to send its genes on to future generations is to turn out offspring that live long enough to reproduce in their turn.

Individual survival is at best just a means to that end. Songbirds rarely survive in the wild for more than a small portion of their possible lifespans. The average life expectancy of a wild Black-capped Chickadee is only two and a half years, but one wild bird lived at least twelve years and five months. My friend Barry Kent MacKay, whose paintings decorate these pages, rescued a Baltimore Oriole, Rory, who lived in his house for an amazing twenty-four years and ten months. In the wild, an oriole might be lucky to last four or five. Larger songbirds may do better; Superb Lyrebirds have lived twenty years in the wild. In general, songbirds in Australia and southern Africa tend to survive longer than their northern counterparts, probably because most of them do not have to deal with harsh winters and long migratory journeys.

Almost everything songbirds are, or do, is the result of an evolutionary winnowing process.

This wild Baltimore
Oriole is unlikely to
live as long as Barry
Kent MacKay's pet,
Rory, who reached his
twenty-fifth birthday.
A wild oriole may
expect to live no
more than four or
five years.

Traits that help to carry on their genes have been kept, and those that do not have been discarded. Even passing on genes may not be enough. They must be passed on more successfully than those of other species, or of other individuals of one's own species—including the genes of one's own mate. The solutions to the environmental, and social, challenges songbirds must meet, not just to survive that process but to emerge triumphant from it, have determined their structure, their behavior, and the daily patterns of their lives.

Their first challenge is to survive and to function. Songbird bodies literally operate at fever pitch. Their body temperature hovers at around 104 degrees Fahrenheit (40°C)—about as hot as it can get without cooking a bird's own proteins. This racing metabolism suits the speed and energy of their lives, but running such a highly tuned machine has a cost. That cost is the need to provide large amounts of fuel. Any animal that small that keeps its temperature that high must eat every day to get enough energy to keep functioning. Birds the size of a chickadee burn more than a gram of fat per day. They cannot stop eating on days when the weather is bad. In fact, they may need to feed more than ever on cold days.

A Black-capped Chickadee can change its body chemistry to adjust for hard times. As winter approaches, its ability to store fat increases—a necessity as it faces colder, shorter days when food is less available and there is less time to find it. Like other north temperate tits, it can dial down its metabolism to save energy during long winter nights, lowering its body temperature by forty-five to fifty-five degrees Fahrenheit (8 to 12°C). So can sunbirds that live in the alpine zone of east African mountains, eleven thousand feet (3350 m) above sea level. When food is scarce, even the tropical Red-capped and Golden-collared Manakins let their temperatures fall by fifty degrees Fahrenheit (10°C) at night, saving about 50 percent of the energy they would otherwise burn as they sleep.

American Goldfinches alter their metabolism in winter to become more heat-efficient. A winter Goldfinch can maintain its body temperature for six to eight hours at minus ninety degrees Fahrenheit (−70°C). A summer bird would not last for more than an hour at these temperatures. In the Arctic, tits, Lapland Longspurs, Snow Buntings, and redpolls burrow into the snow at (opposite) The Blackburnian Warbler shares the northern North American spruce forests with another warbler species. In a classic study, Robert MacArthur showed that each species tends to hunt in its own distinctive corner of the trees. The Blackburnian forages high in the outer crown.

night to escape the winter cold. In western Maine, Golden-crowned Kinglets weighing just under a quarter of an ounce (5–6 g) must manage even when the winter mercury plunges to minus twenty-two degrees Fahrenheit (–30°C). Kinglets, Winter Wrens, Brown Creepers and European Treecreepers, Long-tailed Tits, and Bushtits huddle together for warmth in winter roosts. The need to roost can be so great that it is worth risking a bird's life. The ornithologist Owen Knorr once found more than a hundred Pygmy Nuthatches huddled in the cavity of a pine tree. The birds were so closely packed together that some had suffocated.

Desert birds face the opposite problem. They must avoid dehydrating in the high heat of midday. Verdins and Black-tailed Gnatcatchers in the Sonoran Desert pass the noon hour resting quietly at specially selected sites in the deepest shade they can find.

Finding the food songbirds need takes energy in itself. A bird has to get more energy from its food than it uses up finding it. Songbirds must, therefore, budget the time and energy they spend foraging. To get the maximum benefit for the least amount of effort, birds have to have, hard-wired into their brains, the ability to construct what zoologists call an *optimal foraging strategy*. How far is it worth flying, for example, to get from one food source to the next? Is it better to take time to eat low-quality food, or to pass it up and search for something better?

White Wagtails prefer medium-sized flies to large ones. Larger flies take longer to catch and swallow, and the energy the wagtails use up in chasing and subduing them more than makes up for any gain from the extra meat. On the other hand, Northwestern Crows prefer big whelks to small ones. The crows get at the whelks, which are a kind of large snail, by dropping them on rocks over and over again. In this case, it takes as much work to break open a small whelk as a large one, and the extra effort simply isn't worth it for whelks below a certain size.

An efficient foraging strategy has to be able to adjust as the seasons change and different sorts of foods become more or less available. If food is scarce, Great Tits will eat pretty much anything they can find. As food becomes more available, however, they begin to ignore foods that are less nutritious or harder to eat, even if they are abundant.

What a bird is able to eat and where it goes to find it may depend on what and where other birds are eating. Several species of insect-eating wood warblers live together in North American spruce forests, each in a distinctive corner where it concentrates its efforts. Bay-breasted and Blackburnian Warblers hunt for food high in the trees, but the Bay-breasted stays near the trunk, while the Blackburnian explores the outer branches. Lower down in the trees, Cape May and Black-throated Green Warblers do the same thing, the former near the trunk and the latter amid the foliage. Below all of them, the Yellow-rumped Warbler searches through the shrubbery. In British forests, where there are no wood warblers,

Great Tits feed on or near the ground, Marsh Tits on large branches, and Blue Tits on smaller twigs.

Are birds like this staying in their particular corners because the other species are there? Evidence from island birds suggests that they are. In the Pacific Northwest of the United States, Black-capped Chickadees live in broad-leaved forests and Chestnut-backed Chickadees in coniferous forest. On the San Juan Islands off the coast, there are no Black-capped Chickadees and the Chestnut-backed lives in both types of forest. On the mainland, it seems, each species can exclude the other from a habitat that could support either one.

In winter, migrant songbirds may change the means they use to stay out of one another's way. Eastern and Western Wood-Pewees, which rarely meet on their breeding grounds, both head for the Andes of South America for the winter. Here, the Eastern Wood-Pewee seems to stay in the highlands over four thousand feet (1200 m), while the Western Wood-Pewee winters in the lowlands of the western Amazon basin. Along the foothills of the eastern Andes in Peru, Cerulean Warblers winter from two to four thousand feet (650–1200 m), but above that they are replaced by Blackburnian Warblers.

Migrants may avoid competing with tropical residents, as well. In central Panama, migrant thrushes, wood warblers, and tyrant flycatchers tend to concentrate on hard-bodied, small insects such as beetles or ants that are too low in nutritional value to interest residents, or on millipedes that are avoided by the locals because they produce distasteful or toxic chemicals.

Insect-eating birds are not the only ones to divide up their environments among themselves. In the New World Tropics, tanagers, which take their fruits while perched, may be eating different fruits from manakins, which pluck theirs in hovering flight.

Over time, species may change physically to avoid competing. Three hundred years ago a violent volcanic eruption destroyed all life on Long Island, a tiny spot of land between New Guinea and New Britain in the southwest Pacific. Today, birds have returned to Long, including two species of small honeyeater, the Ebony and Scarlet-bibbed Myzomelas. In less than three centuries, the Ebony Myzomela has become larger than its ancestor, while the Scarlet-bibbed has grown smaller. On a small island with limited resources, the two species may have become as different as possible from each other in order to live together.

This sort of habitat division allows different species of songbirds to divide up their living space among themselves. For an individual competing with other members of its own species, though, the only solution may be to stake out its own exclusive feeding area and defend it against all comers. That is one reason songbirds establish territories, but it is not the only one. A territory is an expression both of a bird's need to survive and of its drive to reproduce.

A territory is any area that a bird defends against rivals. It can be simply an area around a female or around a choice source of food. For most songbirds, though, a territory has to be big enough to provide all the things—a good supply of food for itself and its family, a suitable place to nest—that its defender needs to survive and to reproduce. Competition for territories may be high, with dominant birds—usually older, more experienced males—getting the best spots. A prime territory may be a dominant male's best signal to a female that he is the one she should choose for her mate.

It takes energy and work to defend a territory, so there is no advantage to a bird in defending a bigger territory than it needs. If plenty of food is available, birds will usually defend smaller areas.

In Australia, New Holland Honeyeater territories shrink when the nectar-rich grevilleas bloom, but grow again when the birds must depend on the nectar supplied by the less productive banksias. The Australian ornithologist David Paton tried to see what would happen if he added extra sugar water to the flowers. The birds, with extra food available, no longer needed to defend such a large area. They shrank their territories to match. It was, as zoologist John Alcock put it, "as if the birds had little calculators in their heads."

Territory size may depend on how many rivals are in the neighborhood. This affects not only how much land a bird can claim, but how much energy it needs to devote to holding on to its property. When American Tree Sparrow populations are low, birds can manage territories so large that they need to use only 20 percent of their living space. As the population grows, the sparrows pack their territories closer together as they run out of elbow room.

Young birds take second place to their elders when it comes to parceling out prime territories. When populations are high, there may not be enough land to go around. Those left out may join the ranks of the *floaters*, living quietly and unobtrusively in the territories of established males. They do not sing or display aggressively, so they can survive in a territory without being expelled by the owner.

In one population of Rufous-collared Sparrows, half the males were floaters, living in a sparrow "underworld" with territories and boundaries of its own. Even among these seemingly unaggressive birds, there were dominant individuals and subordinate ones, with the dominant birds getting the better spots. If one of the birds holding a real territory died or disappeared, a dominant male from the floater population quickly took over.

In some songbirds, females defend territories of their own. Both male and female Superb Lyrebirds, for example, defend territories, with a male overlapping the territories of up to six females.

The Rufous-collared Sparrow is a common and familiar bird throughout Central and South America. In some places, as many as half of the sparrows in a population may be "floaters," living unobtrusive lives within the territories of older or more dominant birds.

In winter, instead of defending a territory that may not have enough food anyway, birds may be better off gathering in flocks where food is concentrated—at a bird feeder, for instance. However, some birds do defend territory in winter. Dippers may set up winter territories along stretches of a stream. Brown Shrikes establish territories on their wintering grounds in Taiwan. Northern Waterthrushes even set up temporary territories around ponds in Texas, which they use as stopover sites while flying north in spring.

Black-capped Chickadees combine the two strategies. By late summer, they gather into flocks. Each flock sets up a group territory it defends all winter. Great Tits have winter territories, too, but give up defending them on really cold days. This is apparently to save energy, but I understand how they feel.

Some birds defend territories not just against their own kind, but against other species pursuing the same limited supply of food. Red-eyed and Philadelphia Vireos exclude one another from their territories with remarkably similar songs. Golden-winged Sunbirds chase other nectar-feeding birds off their territory, and so will wintering Northern Mockingbirds defending a patch of berry bushes.

New Holland Honeyeaters are too small to chase off Red Wattlebirds, so they flutter at them instead, harassing the larger birds as they try to feed.

Red-winged Blackbirds can breed anywhere Yellow-headed Blackbirds do—but the larger yellowheads usually evict male redwings from their territories when they arrive in the spring. Red-winged Blackbirds, though, have a much wider habitat tolerance than Yellow-headed Blackbirds. Yellowheads stay almost entirely in marshes. They are inhibited by the presence of trees adjacent to their breeding sites. Oddly, the key factor appears to be the angle by which the tops of trees project above the marsh. More than thirty degrees—no yellowheads. Cliffs have the same effect.

The drive to reproduce, for each bird to maximize the potential of his or her own genes, sets up an evolutionary contest between males and females. The more females a male can fertilize, the more young he is likely to produce—but that may not suit the females, because the more help a female

bird gets from her mate, the easier her job of making sure that her young survive will be. A female who mates with more than one male may increase her own chances of producing young with a first-class complement of genes—but that will not suit her mate, because every egg fathered by another male is a lost opportunity to pass on his genes. Besides helping out, he may have to guard her from other males—which, in turn, lowers his own opportunities to mate with other females. The result of this tussle is one or another of a series of possible mating systems. The commonest of these, in songbirds, is monogamy.

Though many songbirds are monogamous for only a season, several European warblers have been known to stay with their mates for at least two nesting cycles. Most Eastern Kingbirds return to the same territory year after year, usually reuniting there with their former mates. Pairs of Rufous Horneros, Brown Cacholotes, and a number of other ovenbirds may stay together for years. Carolina Wrens may mate for life.

This male Yellow-headed Blackbird is in exaggerated display, its harsh croak a warning—both to other male yellowheads and to Red-winged Blackbirds—to stay out of its territory. Yellow-headed Blackbirds chase redwings from their territories, but redwings can set up their own in places yellowheads avoid.

Nine bird species out of ten are monogamous. There is a reason for this. A brood of youngsters demands a tremendous amount of food. If both parents bring food to the chicks, their chances of fledging successfully are usually much better. Nest building or sitting on eggs may be less demanding, but many monogamous males help with these chores, too.

How much the male helps can vary within a single species. Male Red-winged Blackbirds help feed their young in Indiana, where female blackbirds prefer experienced males for their mates. In the state of Washington, males don't help at all, and females don't seem to care whether their mates are experienced or not.

Even among monogamous birds, though, a good deal of what ornithologists delicately call *extra-pair copulation* goes on. To put it bluntly, birds cheat—and, we are now discovering, they cheat a lot.

In Europe, some male Pied Flycatchers, after establishing their main territory, set up side territories to lure in late-arriving females. After a female falls for this and builds her nest, the male abandons her and returns to his prime territory, where he helps to feed his first brood. The females however, may get their revenge. If anything happens to the male, they seduce their neighbors, who end up having to help them feed young that they did not father.

Thirty to 40 percent of the matings in Indigo Buntings are the result of members of a pair stepping out on each other. Perhaps one in five of the matings that male Red-winged Blackbirds get on their territories may not be with their mates, and most Red-winged Blackbird nests contain young whose real fathers are the males in the territories next door. Much of this songbird adultery consists of males pursuing, or even forcing themselves upon, other females, but—as in the Pied Flycatcher—not all. Female Bluethroats pay regular visits to the territories of nearby males before they lay their eggs. They could just be hunting food, but they may be checking out the quality of potential extramarital partners.

Purple Martins are past masters at adultery. These days, Martins usually nest in "apartment buildings" people put up in the vain hope that the birds will eat hordes of mosquitoes. Older, more experienced males arrive early in spring. Once established in the penthouse suites (the hardest for predators to reach), they sing a dawn song that attracts younger males to the colony. Then the older birds force themselves on the younger birds' mates. So successful are the old rakes that yearling males usually father only 29 percent of the birds that their mates rear. With the help of the females on the floors below, an older male can raise his output for the season by another three to four young birds annually. Eugene Morton, who studied this rather scandalous behavior, called it "cuckoldry in the condo."

Female birds may hedge their own bets. In North America, at least one-quarter of migratory songbirds mate before they reach their breeding grounds. Once a pair really does form, it is a wise father that knows his own child.

Males can guard their mates, but this, too, has its costs. Dominant male Yellow-rumped Caciques, large colonial relatives of American orioles, spend so much time and energy guarding their females that they lose weight with age, weaken, and are soon displaced by younger, less preoccupied birds.

If females can raise young without help and guard their nests alone, the pressure keeping males monogamous—or even occasionally bigamous—is off. The result can be any of a series of nonmonogamous mating systems. A few songbirds are *polygynous*, each male having several mates. At least 20 percent of European passerines are regularly polygynous. Willow Warblers are monogamous in some areas, but in others as many as 80 percent of the males may have two or even three mates. Other birds are entirely promiscuous—the birds mate, but do not form any kind of pair bond. Female Nelson's and Saltmarsh Sharp-tailed Sparrows, for example, will solicit matings from many different males. These are not hard-and-fast categories—all sorts of intermediate situations can occur, too.

In the marshes around Lake Neuseidl, Austria, polygynous Great Reed Warblers nest where insects are abundant. Where Moustached and Reed Warblers nest, insects are far less numerous, and both are monogamous. Eleven of the fourteen North American polygynous songbirds breed in marshes. Red-winged Blackbirds nest there amid huge numbers of insects. A female can easily sup-

ply her young alone as this bonanza emerges from the waters—if she is in the right place. A male blackbird holding a prime territory can afford several mates—perhaps five at once, or ten over the course of a season—but a bird on a second-rate territory may be forced into monogamy, even celibacy.

Fruit-eating birds are more likely to be polygynous or promiscuous than insect-eating birds. Fruit is easy to gather, and if the fruits a female brings her young are nutritious enough she may not need her mate's help. The Magnificent Bird-of-Paradise feeds on highly nutritious fruits such as nutmegs, which are hard to open but very rewarding for birds that can manage it. Male Magnificents are promiscuous, and females raise their young alone. The Trumpet Manucode, another bird-of-paradise, feeds on poorer (but less difficult) fruits such as figs. The young need lots of them to grow and both parents have to work to deliver enough of them, and so the Trumpet Manucode has remained monogamous.

Polygynous or promiscuous males need more than just free time. When some males are able to mate with several females, other males may not be able to mate at all. Competition among polygynous males for a female's attention is, therefore, fierce. Combatants need to be aggressive and demonstrative, and the successful ones are literally on steroids. During the breeding season, polygynous males have higher-than-usual levels of testosterone. The hormone really does give the birds an edge—normally monogamous Song and White-throated Sparrows injected with jumped-up levels of testosterone become bigamists. High-testosterone birds are more aggressive, more successful at defending territories and guarding mates. Extra testosterone, though, is only an advantage when polygyny itself is an advantage. Yellow-headed Blackbirds given extra testosterone turned out to be less likely to spend time caring for their young. Though the chemically altered males did attract additional mates, their output of successfully raised young birds ended up being lower than normal. In the wrong circumstances, being a supermale is a bad idea, and that may be why polygyny is rare.

Why should females go along with a polygynous system? Perhaps because, under it, they no longer have to settle for a second-rate male or a poor territory merely because the top spots have been taken. In fact, as we shall see in the next chapter when we look at the extremes to which polygynous males must go to attract mates, their females—who have the power to choose which males get to mate and which do not—are, in some ways, in the driver's seat.

A few songbirds have adopted a particular refinement of a polygynous or promiscuous mating system. Instead of each male establishing a territory and pursuing females on his own, the males congregate at a communal display ground called a *lek*. Lekking songbirds include five tyrant flycatchers, eighteen cotingas, twenty-four manakins, (probably) the four asities, the two lyrebirds, twenty-eight birds-of-paradise, four whydahs, Jackson's Widowbird, and the Yellow-whiskered Greenbul.

A lek may be a single tree full of madly dancing Raggiana Birds-of-Paradise, or simply an area with a number of males on separate display grounds, but reasonably close to one another. Male blue-backed manakins of the genus *Chiroxiphia* actually dance with each other, leapfrogging over each other's backs at the climax of their display. Male *Chiroxiphia* manakins are splendid creatures, with bright-red crowns, turquoise mantles, and, for some, central tail feathers lengthened into spikes, points, or streamers. The males have a strong dominance relationship with one another, and no male has a chance of mating unless he reaches at least a beta status. That can take eight years, a very long time for such a small bird. In a four-year study of the Long-tailed Manakin, only eight of out of eight-five males achieved any copulations at all. One male was responsible for 67 percent of all matings.

When a female bird visits a lek, she cannot be looking for a rich territory, because the male she chooses won't have one. She can't be searching for the mate that will best help feed her young

(opposite) The males of the polygynous birds-of-paradise may be free from the duties of rearing their young, but they are locked in an evolutionary race to lure potential mates with ever more spectacular displays and exaggerated plumage. This male Ribbon-tailed Astrapia, from the mountain forests of central New Guinea, carries the longest tail feathers of any songbird.

Two male Long-tailed
Manakins leapfrog
over each other as
they display to a
female visiting a lek
at Monteverde,
Costa Rica.

or build her nest, because he won't do any of those things. She is, in fact, only after his body. Or, more precisely, his genes.

That is why, in almost every case, she will ignore most of the eagerly dancing suitors and concentrate on the male at the top of the heap. One lek of the Lesser Bird-of-Paradise held seven males, but while observers were watching it, out of twenty-five matings they recorded, one male made twenty-four of them. Why, then, would the other males bother to show up at the lek at all? Why risk comparison with the best of the bunch?

It may simply be that since the females are searching out the best males, a subordinate male's only chance of running across one in the right sort of circumstances is to be where that male is. He may at least have some chance of getting a mating now and then. Among birds-of-paradise, to lek or not to lek may depend on how the females behave. If females range widely looking for food, and overlap one another's hunting grounds—as they do in such lekking species as the Raggiana Bird-of-Paradise and Lawes' Parotia—a lek site could be visited by large numbers of them. If, on the other hand, each female forages in a small area exclusive to her alone, as in the Magnificent Bird-of-Paradise and the Buff-tailed Sicklebill, a lek at one site would be pointless, as only one or two females could visit it and the rest would miss it altogether.

For a maelstrom of sexual politics, shifting relationships, and soap-opera mating scenarios, consider the Dunnock. If there is a mating system in existence, the Dunnock, a common garden bird in Europe, has probably tried it. The same bird may be monogamous one year, polygynous the next, or even polyandrous—several males mating with and cooperating with a single female.

Beneath this plain exterior lurks a bird with one of the most complicated and variable sex lives ever studied: the Dunnock, or Hedgesparrow, of Europe. Both male and female Dunnocks may have one, two, or several mates, and may change whatever sexual arrangement they have from one year to the next.

Before Nicholas Davies began his study of Dunnocks, no one suspected that songbirds could adopt this sort of fluid arrangement, which at its extreme becomes *polygynandry*—each sex having several mates. Polygynandry turns out, though, to be more common than we thought. Similar systems have turned up in the Dunnock's close relatives, the Japanese and Alpine Accentors, and in more distantly related birds: Smith's Longspurs, Superb Fairy-Wrens, Aquatic Warblers, and Stitchbirds.

As the avian adultery record demonstrates, mating does not end competition among males. It continues with particular ferocity among polygynandrous birds. When one of the males copulates, he is not only depositing his sperm. He may be flushing out, or at least diluting, the sperm of the last male on the scene, increasing the chance that his sperm rather than his rival's will fertilize her. Since the female has a number of potential mates, every male will try to be last at the post, no matter how many matings it takes. Before she lays her eggs, a female Smith's Longspur mates an average of seven times an hour with up to three different males, for an average of 365 copulations per season. Male longspurs have greatly enlarged testes, and no wonder. Before a male Dunnock mates, he pecks at the opening of his female's *cloaca* (a common opening for the genital and digestive tracts, lovingly named from the Latin word for sewer), causing her to eject a droplet of sperm from her last copulation. Splendid and White-winged Fairy-Wrens have testes that make up 10 percent of their body weight and a special cloacal protuberance to store sperm— a combination allowing them to deliver 8.3 billion sperm in a single copulation. Human males, by contrast, have to get by with about 400 million.

A brood of Aquatic Warblers may be fostered by as many as four different males, a record among birds. Aquatic Warblers enjoy the longest copulations known in the bird world—an average of twenty-four minutes each, compared with one or two seconds for most songbirds. These long sessions may be a way for a male to keep a female away from his rivals.

The Stitchbird, or Hihi, is a rare honeyeater from New Zealand; it has been extinct on the main islands for about a century. For decades it survived only on Little Barrier, a tiny but fascinating island in Hauraki Gulf, where I met it in 1974. Today, conservationists have established populations on other islands, including Kapiti off the South Island in 1991 and 1992. Here, out of thirty-four nests studied in 1994, twenty-two were tended by monogamous pairs, four were the result of polygyny, three of polyandry, and one of polygynandry. The Stitchbird has the distinction of being the only bird known to copulate face to face. They do mate in the usual way, with the male mounting on the female's back, but face-to-face mating seems to be a form of rape. It may start with up to five males chasing a female to the ground. Its purpose, again, may be sperm competition—the attempt by each male to make sure his sperm, and not his rival's, fertilizes her eggs.

The factor driving all this may be the need not for sex, but for food. Male and female Dunnocks both defend overlapping territories. In average times, male and female territories stay roughly the same size, overlapping on a one-on-one basis, and the birds stay monogamous. If the leaf litter is thick with the tiny beetles, springtails, spiders, and other creatures Dunnocks eat, females can afford smaller territories. Male territories will stay large enough to overlap one or more

The endangered Stitchbird of New Zealand is the only bird known to copulate face-to-face. It gets its name not from any sewing ability, but from its call note, whlch sounds vaguely like the word "stitch." This is a male.

territories of the females, letting them be at least bigamists if they can. If food is scarce, though, female territories grow until each has swept up more than one of the males. Now they not only have larger areas to find food, they have more males to help them—a distinct advantage in hard times. Under really harsh conditions, males may need to cooperate with a mate they all share to be sure that their own young, even if they share a nest with half siblings, have a chance to survive. So the swing in Dunnock lifestyles from males with female harems, to proper monogamous family units, to females with male harems, depends on how many six- or eight-legged creatures happen to be crawling around in the leaf litter where they forage. The twin drives, to survive and reproduce, have converged yet again.

FIELD GUIDES AND MORE

Whenever interesting birds landed in the schoolyard, my fourth-grade teacher, Miss Wood, stopped the class and sent us to the window to see. How did she know what they were? I asked her. She showed me, in reply, a magical book called a "Peterson." It had pictures of every kind of bird imaginable, beautifully painted and neatly arranged. Little arrows pointed to features of the bird that could help to identify it. The book called them *field marks*. Like so many others, thanks to Peterson's *A Field Guide to the Birds*, I was hooked.

Roger Tory Peterson, who was a friendly and fascinating man, died just as I began to write this book. His first field guide, published in 1934, gave us the birds. It proved that nature could be enjoyed in some other way than down the barrel of a gun. I think it is the most valuable conservation tool ever invented, though it really isn't about wildlife conservation at all.

Today, there are field guides for almost every country in the world. With a pair of good binoculars, a field guide is the most essential purchase you can make as a birder (and don't forget field guides to other animals and plants, too—birds aren't the only things out there). The big question for many people, now that Peterson's guides are not the only ones on the shelf, is which one to buy.

The best solution is to have more than one. If you are planning to buy only one field guide, though, do not choose one illustrated with photographs. Photographs can be quite misleading. Tricks of light and shadow can change the very features you need to check for identification. A field guide illustrated with paintings does not have this problem, and the birds can be arranged and posed in the most useful way possible. A guide illustrated with photographs makes a nice backup, but your primary guide should be illustrated by a good artist. The Peterson and *National Geographic* guides are still North American birders' most popular choices.

One of the most important things you can do with a field guide, whichever one you select, is to use it before you go into the field. Spend time studying the plates. Learn what to look for. Try to make yourself as familiar as possible if not with the details of each species, at least with the different bird groups. This is not just to show off to other birders when you finally do go out. Birds don't always let you get either a good look or a long look. If you already know what field marks to look for and what they mean, you are more likely to get the most out of your encounters, however brief. Besides, you will have to spend less time fumbling with your guide in the field if you already know where to look for the birds you want to identify. Some people find it useful to mark the major bird groups in their guides with index tabs, and you can even buy specially made ones for this purpose.

If you can locate one for your area, a bird-finding guide can be very useful. This is a book that tells you where to go to see birds and what kinds of birds you can expect to find there, and it usually gives directions for getting to the right spot. A good bird-finding guide should include a checklist telling you what species occur in your area, and when. You may also want a separate checklist card, which can be useful for recording your own observations. Bird-finding guides can, as well, be a great help in planning weekend excursions or longer vacation trips. You can also find bird-finding holiday ideas in magazines such as *Birder's World*.

Of course, *really* modern birders don't have to look at birds at all. There are enough Web sites, Internet news groups, CD-ROMs, and software programs for birders to keep any songbird hacker happy. The Internet is rapidly becoming one of the best sources for bird-related information. The World Wide Web has pages with advice on everything from how to build a birdhouse to where to watch birds in Indonesia. An excellent place to start is at the Birding on the Web page at http://www.birder.com/. See "Cyber-Birding" at the back of this book for more.

FOUR

FINE FEATHERS

Seven years, some say, these green-brown birds
elect blue for their colour
and dance for it, their eyes round as the sea's horizons,
blue as grape-hyacinths.

And when those seven years are served?
See, there he flies, the old one,
the male made perfect—
black in the shadow, but in the caressing sun
bluer, more royal than the ancient sea.

—JUDITH WRIGHT, *SATIN BOWER-BIRDS*

Cedar Waxwing tails are normally tipped with a bright yellow band. Recently, birds with orange bands, like the one on the left, have been seen in the northeastern United States. The change appears to be caused by pigments absorbed from a new item in the birds' diet, a Japanese honeysuckle.

A bird's feathers outweigh its skeleton. Songbirds may sport from two to four thousand of them. On wings and tail, their shape and arrangement determine how well, how far, and with how much maneuverability they can fly. The contour feathers that cover their bodies give them shape and color. Beneath the contour feathers lies a layer of insulating down. Its thickness is determined by where birds live—arctic finches have much heavier coats of down than do tropical birds.

A typical feather consists of a shaft, or *rachis*, lined on either side with barbs that, in turn, link to one another with hooklike *barbules*. Down feathers lack both the projecting shaft and the hooks, leaving the barbs to fluff out into a cottony, insulating puff.

Bristles are highly modified feathers, usually with no barbs at all. A bird's eyelashes are bristles. Crows have bristles over their nostrils to protect their bills. Long rictal bristles on either side of their bills were once thought to help flycatchers sweep up insects, but cutting off the bristles seems to have no effect on a Willow Flycatcher's ability to catch flies. They may, instead, protect its eyes as it darts into the path of its prey.

The Hooded Pitohui of New Guinea was the first bird found to have poisonous feathers. Its striking color pattern may be a warning to potential predators.

Woodcreepers, barbtails, and northern treecreepers—but not Australian treecreepers—use stiffened tail feathers to brace themselves against trunks and limbs. The pitohuis of New Guinea—with one other New Guinea songbird, the Blue-capped Ifrit, and possibly a few South American birds—have poisonous feathers. Three species carry a nerve poison in their feathers, skin, and muscles that is basically the same as the toxin in the skin of poison dart frogs. The most strikingly patterned pitohui, the Hooded, with its black, crested head, black wings and tail, and bright rufous body, is also the most toxic—one of the few birds to wear warning colors. The local people of New Guinea have known for a long time that eating a pitohui will make you sick, and have developed special ways to prepare them.

As often as once per hour, birds run their feathers through their beaks, combing and re-arranging the barbs and sweeping off more obvious parasites. This wash-and-brush-up operation is called *preening*. To make preening even more effective, a special gland just above the tail, the *uropygial*, or preen gland, secretes a rich mixture of oil, waxes, and fats that keeps the feathers moist and flexible and may get rid of fungi, feather lice, and feather-digesting bacteria. Members of a pair often preen each other, a behavior known as *allopreening*.

When there isn't time to preen, birds scratch. That helps get rid of feather lice, too. Birds that have had the misfortune to lose one leg, and cannot scratch, may become infested with them.

Birds scratch in two ways, either under the wing or, in a more contortionist mode, by reaching over the wing with one leg. The type of scratching seems to depend on the species. Some wood warblers scratch directly—that is, under the wing—while others scratch indirectly—or over the wing.

A Worm-eating Warbler preens its feathers, passing them through its beak and rearranging the barbs, in a ritual practiced by all living birds.

One peculiar type of feather care seems restricted to songbirds. Many species—well over two hundred are known—will stroke their plumage with ants, or lie spread-eagled in an ant colony and allow the insects to invade their feathers. We are still not sure why birds indulge in *anting*, as this behavior is called, but the formic acid secreted by the insects may act as an insecticide, helping the birds get rid of feather parasites. Sometimes birds will ant without ants, using bits of orange peel, or even smoke. I once watched a Long-tailed Cinclodes doing something like anting on a patch of bare ground on the Brazilian planalto. It lay down on one side and spread out its uppermost wing, then ruffled its feathers and began to preen, but did not seem to be picking up any ants; perhaps the insects were crawling through its feathers unaided.

In late summer, a bird's plumage may be studded with growing *pin feathers*, their barbs protected by a temporary sheath. It may be missing wing and tail feathers, too. These are signs that the bird is in *molt*. Molt is the process by which a bird completely, or nearly completely, replaces its feathers with a new set.

A songbird in molt sheds and regrows the equivalent of about 12 percent of its weight at least once, and often twice, a year. This may seem wasteful, but it is quite necessary. A worn, broken, or damaged feather cannot be repaired—only replaced. Since birds depend on their wing and tail feathers to fly, they cannot afford to have them in poor condition. Molt provides them with a fresh set.

Birds can be plagued by feather lice and mites. Molt sheds both the feathers and their unwanted passengers. Nelson's and Saltmarsh Sharp-tailed Sparrows, which molt twice a year, end up with fewer parasites living in their feathers than do Seaside Sparrows, which molt once.

Many songbirds go through a second molt before the breeding season to take on the bright colors they display in their quests for territories or mates, though some birds change their appearance without molting. A European Starling loses its winter spots by the time the breeding season comes along—but the feathers have not been replaced. Instead, they have worn down, and the spots, which were on the tips of the feathers, have been abraded.

There are other reasons for molting twice a year. Some African larks live in windy deserts where their feathers can be literally sandblasted away. They need two sets of feathers a year to handle the onslaught.

A double molt gives birds an opportunity to add a thicker layer of feather insulation in the fall and get rid of it again in the spring. House Sparrows almost double their plumage weight in fall, going from three-tenths to one-half an ounce (8–14 g) of fresh plumage.

The timing of molt is governed by a hormonal calendar that uses a special receptor in the midbrain to translate changes in day length into signals to the pituitary gland. Since hormones also control a bird's urge to breed or migrate, its hormonal calendar makes sure that these important events happen at the right time and in the right order. Adult songbirds usually molt right after the breeding season and before migration, though some young Blue Tits migrate before their molt is finished.

Molting takes energy, but how much difference this makes per day depends on how quickly the bird sheds and regrows its feathers. Some Eurasian songbirds burn their metabolic furnaces at from 8 to 50 percent higher when in molt. Brown-headed Cowbirds in molt use up to 24 percent more oxygen than normal. Most molting birds, however, simply lower their daily activity, both to save energy and—perhaps more important—to protect their growing feathers.

In the Arctic, where spring and summer may last only a few weeks, Lapland Longspurs have to molt very quickly. Snow Buntings may shed half of their wing feathers at once, rendering them flightless for a week or two. Tropical birds, by contrast, can stretch out their molt, sometimes for an entire year.

Wing and tail feathers must be in good shape for any substantial journey, even for tropical dry-country species that simply wander when food is scarce. Some Australian finches can go through a quick molt before they need to shift to a new area. Nomadic starlings like the Rosy Starling can interrupt their molt before setting off. Desert birds may need to wait for the rare rains before they can breed. If the rains come while they are in molt, they can stop molting and breed while times are good.

Leaves look green because they are full of pigment. The blue of the sky is a structural color— the molecules of gas in the atmosphere scatter the sun's light like tiny prisms. Iridescent or glossy colors, such as the colors on an oil slick, are structural, too.

Songbird feathers contain both pigmented and structural colors. They carry a range of pigments in their feathers: black, brownish or reddish melanins, red or yellow carotenoids, and purplish porphyrins. Melanins packed into wing and tail feathers make them harder, stronger, and better able to withstand abrasion and the rigors of flight—which may be one reason why many brightly

A Snow Bunting in non-breeding plumage blends with the white of the winter snow.

colored birds, such as the Scarlet Tanager, have dark wing feathers. Melanins also concentrate heat, and help feathers to dry more rapidly.

Songbird colors may depend on where the pigments are. Red Crossbills look brick-red because they have pigment in both the barbs and barbules of their feathers. White-winged Crossbills have the same pigment, but only in the barbs. Light glinting off their translucent barbules combines with the red pigment to make a White-winged Crossbill in fresh plumage look pink instead of red. As its plumage wears down and the barbules are eroded, the bird gets redder and redder.

The blue of a bluebird or an Indigo Bunting is a structural color, the result of melanin particles in its barbs that scatter short-wave blue light the way the molecules in the sky do. So are the brilliant iridescent colors of grackles, sunbirds, and glossy starlings.

Some colors, especially greens or violets, combine pigment and structure. The rich violet of the South American Pompadour Cotinga is produced by a mixture of red carotenoids and structural blues.

Songbird color patterns can be a matter of simple genetics. The stripes on the head of both male and female White-throated Sparrows can be either white or tan, depending on which version of a specific chromosome they happen to carry. The Gouldian Finch comes in three color forms: red-faced, black-faced, and (more rarely) yellow-faced. Several Eurasian and North African wheatears also come in more than one color scheme.

For many songbirds, the adult plumage pattern depends on whether they are male or female. *Sexual plumage dimorphism*, as this difference is called, has arisen, or disappeared again once it has developed, at least 150 times in songbirds. Though it has usually arisen because the male has developed bright colors or ornaments, it can be lost either by the male reverting to female-type plumage (as in some West Indian tanagers) or by the female becoming as distinctive as the male (as in the White-capped Water-Redstart). The Plumbeous Water-Redstart may have started out sexually dimorphic, gone through a stage in which the female resembled the male, and then developed a new, duller look for the female based on the immature plumage.

The scholar Udo Savalli recently reviewed thirty different explanations for the colors and feather shapes of birds: suggestions that dark colors may protect birds against ultraviolet radiation, proposals that eye stripes might help hunting birds to sight on their prey, theories that involve signaling to other birds, or even other animals, even notions that some extreme variations may have no function at all. No one, simple, neat explanation fits all the patterns, colors, crests, plumes, streamers, fans, wires, fringes, and other ornaments that decorate the world's songbirds.

Probably the most important function for songbird colors is camouflage—think of all those "little green jobs" and "little brown jobs." The colors of many desert birds match the soil. In South Africa, Spike-heeled Larks vary in color from place to place, depending on the color of the earth, and the little-known Red Lark is confined to the red dunes of the northern Cape. The Desert Lark of North Africa, Leconte's Thrasher of the American Southwest, and the Gibberbird of Australia can be hard to see against the pale, sandy background where they live. It's not hard to imagine why the Snow Bunting is mostly white, especially if you have watched drifting flocks of "snowflakes" swirling among their icy namesakes over a frozen field. Its close relative, McKay's Bunting, which never leaves the High North at all, is even whiter.

Dark feathers in front of the eyes of many insect-eating birds may cut down glare that could interfere with their eyesight. Like the blacking an athlete smears under his eyes to help him see, dark feathers may help make their owner keener-eyed, and therefore a better hunter.

A few birds mimic the patterns of other species. Several orioles from the Lesser Sunda Islands of Indonesia look—and act—almost exactly like large aggressive members of the honeyeater family called friarbirds. Friarbirds tend to chase other species of birds away from fruiting trees they control, and perhaps the mimicry of the oriole allows it to join the friarbirds and get a meal.

Many songbirds complement their feather patterns with bright colors on their bills, legs, patches of bare skin, or the irides of their eyes. Many male birds-of-paradise add brightly colored mouth linings to the list of ornaments they display to a female. Bare facial skin can range from a tiny patch near the eye to the entirely bald head of the Noisy Friarbird (hence its name) or the grotesque, pendulous ornaments decorating a male Wattled Starling in breeding plumage. The Smoky Honeyeater of New Guinea sports a large, bare yellow patch around its eye that has one feature feathers lack—it can change color, blushing deep red when the bird is excited.

That is not to say that feathers lack expression. Wing bars can be flashed, tails spread and twitched. An aggressive Steller's Jay will raise its crest; one that is about to retreat will lower it.

Some birds keep patches of bright color concealed until they are needed. Many antshrikes have a patch of white feathers on their backs that they expose only if threatened. Tyrant flycatchers often have hidden crown patches of orange, red, yellow, or white. The ruby crown of a Ruby-crowned Kinglet or the yellow tufts on the chest of the Malachite Sunbird normally remain tucked out of sight, flashed only in moments of aggressive display or, perhaps, to confuse an enemy.

The ultimate in hidden ornaments belongs to the Royal Flycatcher. On rare occasions when a Royal Flycatcher is sufficiently excited or threatened, it opens what normally seems to be simply a narrow brownish crest, spreading it forward into a great fan of red feathers (yellow in the female), tipped and spotted with iridescent blue, splaying from side to side over its bill.

An alarmed Royal Flycatcher fans its crest, gapes to reveal its orange mouth lining, and transforms itself into one of the most garish of songbirds.

As the fan billows outward, the flycatcher gapes, revealing the orange lining of its mouth, and sways its head slowly from side to side. The transformation is astonishing—more than enough to startle a rival or a predator.

Most commonly, however, bright colors function in display—they establish a bird's social status among members of its own sex or demand the attention of the other. There is no simple way to tell, though, whether the bright colors and baroque ornaments of many male songbirds are there to impress a female, to challenge another male, or for some other reason altogether. You have to watch what the birds are doing, or even manipulate the system a bit with experiments.

A male Red-winged Blackbird flashes his wing shoulders as he proclaims his territory in early spring.

Female Red-winged Blackbirds are not lured in with bright red shoulders. Their concern is to select mates that have managed to take over high-quality territories, with good places to put nests, water nearby, and lots of food in the area. A male's epaulettes are part of a game of bluff among rivals, each seeking to stake his claim to the kind of territory females want. Males arrive on the breeding grounds ahead of the females, where they posture, sing their loud *onk-areee* songs, and generally try to elbow one another out of the way. The epaulettes are not passive armaments. Their owner covers and uncovers them, flashing them like signal lights. If the bird is aggressive, he can expose his red shoulders completely. If he is not defending his territory and wants to avoid being harassed by other birds, he tucks them out of sight. The epaulettes are crucial for this contest. When scientists trapped some Red-winged Blackbird males and painted the red epaulettes black, other males quickly pushed them off their territories—even though the painted birds were just as noisy and aggressive as they had been before.

The breeding-plumaged male Long-tailed Widowbird, an African weaver, looks rather like a Red-winged Blackbird, except that it trails an extraordinary tail over a foot and a half (0.5 m) long. As it flies over the grass tops, its tail shudders and flutters behind it in spectacular display. No less a naturalist than Charles Darwin noted in *The Origin of Species* that a female Long-tailed Widowbird will "disown" a male "robbed of the long tail-feathers with which he is ornamented during the breeding season."

Long-tailed Widowbirds were obvious choices for interfering scientists eager to try experiments. Malte Andersson lengthened some widowbird tails and shortened others. This may sound something like the Red-winged Blackbird experiments—but the results were completely different. A longer or shorter tail seems to have nothing to do with a Long-tailed Widowbird's ability to hold on to a territory, but it does affect how many females he manages to attract. The longer the tail, the more successful the suitor.

So, it seems, female blackbirds choose territories, while female widowbirds plump for plumage. Not quite. In the Yellow-shouldered Widowbird, another long-tailed species subjected to shortening experiments, males with artificially shortened tails had trouble getting a territory, but had no trouble mating once they did. Female Yellow-shouldered Widowbirds, like Red-winged Blackbirds, are more interested in real estate than in fancy feathers.

In an aviary experiment, not only did female Shaft-tailed Whydahs—still another long-tailed African finch—prefer males with artificially lengthened tail plumes, but the males displayed and sang more than their normal rivals. The males may simply have been responding to the greater amount of attention they got from the females—something that happens in humans, too.

Female choice seems to have been behind the development of the tail streamers of Barn Swallows and Scarlet-tufted Malachite Sunbirds. Male-male competition has produced the wing bars of the Yellow-browed Warbler and the black bib of the House Sparrow. To make things even more confusing, the yellow head of the Yellow-headed Blackbird and the brilliant orange of the Baltimore Oriole do not seem to have anything to do with either one. If this doesn't suggest much of a pattern to you, you are not alone.

Why should a female bird select her mate on the basis of extravagant plumage or wild displays? Is she simply responding to the dictates of genetic fashion, like a bar habituée who selects her partner on the basis of dancing style rather than on earning capacity or character? Or do the differences among displaying males somehow tell her which male is most likely to give her fit offspring?

Fancy feathers in good condition may be a sign of a healthier potential mate. Barn Swallows are plagued with bloodsucking mites. A bird with a heavy mite infestation cannot grow as long a set of tail plumes as a bird with fewer parasites. Swallows huddle together in their nests, and a male with a lot of parasites will probably end up sharing them with his mate. By choosing a male with a longer tail, the female reduces her own chances of ending up in poor health.

House Finches vary from pale yellow to bright red. Their color comes from carotenoid pigments. Animals cannot produce carotenoids—reds, oranges, and yellows—in their bodies, but must get them from their food. Cedar Waxwings in eastern North America, for example, have started to show up with orange, rather than yellow, tail bands, apparently because they are picking up a particular carotenoid from the berries of a Japanese honeysuckle that is now common there. A red House Finch's brilliance depends on its access to the right foods at molting time, and its brightness may therefore be a real indicator of its survival abilities. Brighter-colored male House Finches are more attentive to their offspring than duller birds. They seem to survive longer, too. Females prefer brightly colored males, and it appears they have good reason to do so.

The use of feathers in display reaches its peak among the stiffly competing males of polygynous or promiscuous birds. Of these, none are more ornate than the polygynous birds-of-paradise. The evolution of ever more fantastic plumage in these birds has produced some feathers that are unique. The central tail feathers of the male Red Bird-of-Paradise have become long, twisting, waxy ribbons emerging from the silky carmine plumes that cascade over his back. The flank feathers of the Twelve-wired Bird-of-Paradise end in wiry projections, six on each side, curving forward toward the bird's head. The male Ribbon-tailed Astrapia earns his name from his two white, black-tipped central tail feathers, the longest of any songbird. The tail of the King Bird-of-Paradise sports long, wirelike streamers that end in round green medallions, formed as the tip of the feather twists around itself like a watch spring. Lawes' Parotia bears six wires on his head, tipped with small feathery disks.

Perhaps the most startling of the lot is one of the smallest, the King of Saxony Bird-of-Paradise. Sprouting from the top of his head are two of the strangest feathers in the entire avian world. Each is an ivory-colored shaft almost twice the length of the bird himself, bearing a series of enamel-like blue lobes. The bird waves them about like semaphore flags, pointing them in all directions as he sings from his treetop perch. Unfortunately for the bird, his plumes are among the most prized decorations worn by tribesmen in the New Guinea highlands.

The male Blue Bird-of-Paradise, his glossy black body set off by an ivory beak, a touch of maroon on the belly, opalescent blue wings, and particularly lovely tufts of filamentous plumes arising from his flanks of rich cobalt blue touched with purple and tipped with pale cinnamon, may be the most beautiful bird in the world. His display has to be seen—and heard—to be believed. When a female arrives at his display post, he lowers himself backward until he is hanging upside down. After a few minutes he shakes out his lacy flank feathers and begins to sway until the plumes become a shimmering, vibrating mass of blue. As his feathers shiver he expands

The strangest display feathers in the bird world, in use: A King of Saxony Bird-of-Paradise waves its enameled head plumes from its perch high in the upland forest of New Guinea's central range.

Is this the most beautiful bird in the world? At the height of his display, a male Blue Bird-of-Paradise hangs upside down and spreads his delicate skirt of blue feathers.

and contracts a black oval patch at their center, calling all the while with a continuous mechanical buzz that sounds something like a pair of electric hair trimmers.

In South America, males of several species of manakin use their feathers for sound, not looks. As they perform their ritual dances, they vibrate stiffened wing feathers that make snapping and cracking noises. The Club-winged Manakin has carried this to an extreme. His inner, or secondary, wing feathers are grossly thickened, twisted, and bent. When the bird flutters his wings during courtship display, they somehow produce a peculiar ringing, metallic noise.

The male Wire-tailed Manakin carries the use of feathers in display to a point approaching S and M. His outer tail feathers end in a cat-o'-nine-tails of long protruding wires. At the height of his dance, as he twists from side to side in front of the female, he brushes them against her throat, switching them back and forth like a miniature flagellant. Experienced females not only accept this, they seem to invite it, approaching in a posture that presents itself for the male's tactile attentions.

The Wire-tailed Manakin's closest relatives, the Crimson-hooded and Band-tailed Manakins, lack the wires but perform the same sort of back-and-forth dance. The display, it seems, came first, and may actually have driven the evolution of the Wire-tailed's whips. The

purpose of the display, after all, is to excite the female, and anything that excites her still more may give the dancing male a special, if slightly kinky, edge.

Though the contest for mates has driven most polygynous birds to develop more and more elaborate feathers, the bowerbirds seem to be in the process not of developing striking plumes and dazzling colors, but of giving them up. In doing so, they have, paradoxically, carried visual displays to an extreme.

The remarkable structures that male bowerbirds build, decorate, repair, and guard for months on end are not nests, or anything like nests. They are, instead, a physical expression of male sexual display.

The catbirds—the only monogamous members of the family, not to be confused with the very different North American catbirds—do not build bowers. All the other bowerbirds are polygynous or promiscuous. The males, who take no part in nesting, devote their full attention to the bower.

The Tooth-billed Bowerbird or Stagemaker clears an area on the forest floor up to ten feet (3 m) in diameter, decorating it with leaves clipped with his tooth-edged bill, and sings from his perch above it. In the rainforests of northern Australia, the Golden Bowerbird constructs an

The display plumes of manakins are for more than looks. The twisted, thickened inner wing feathers of the **Club-winged Manakin** (left) are percussion instruments, and the protruding shafts of the **Wire-tailed Manakin's** tail feathers (right) are flagellant's whips, lashed back and forth across the throat of a willing female.

The enormous maypole bower of the Golden Bowerbird of Australia's northern rainforests, supported by two saplings, dwarfs its builder as he stands on its central display platform.

enormous bower running from one sapling to another, decorated with bits of yellowish lichen that he retrieves from the tops of the forest trees.

In New Guinea, the Golden-crested Bowerbird builds a mat of dead fern stems that may be more than six feet (2 m) across. He decorates the mat with feathers, piles of snail shells, beetle wing cases, tree fungus, fruits, and bits of resin, and drapes the branches above it with orchid stems. When a female visits the mat, he goes through an extraordinary groveling performance, prostrating himself on his mat and shuffling toward her, hissing, spluttering, and occasionally shaking his head until his golden crest becomes a vibrating blur and the fern stems beneath him shudder with his movements.

Of the other bowerbirds, five species assemble twigs around the trunk of a sapling to make a maypole bower, and eight more assemble two rows of parallel, upright twigs (or, in the Spotted Bowerbird, straw) into an avenue bower. Bowerbirds are famous—one could say notorious—for decorating their bowers with anything they can lay their beaks on. One Spotted Bowerbird bower sported a glass eye. Seven of the eight avenue-building bowerbirds, and one maypole builder, even paint the walls of their bower with plant juices, charcoal, mixtures of dried grasses, and saliva.

The male Satin Bowerbird, best-known of the avenue builders, is a large, dark-blue bird with a brilliant azure eye. Individual birds have been recorded occupying a bower site for twenty years. Males may keep using a bower itself for more than thirty years, with new males taking over as old ones die or are displaced. The Satin Bowerbird decorates its bower with any blue object it can find: feathers, ribbons, bottle caps, bits of plastic, berries. Satin Bowerbirds have to learn how to keep up a proper bower. Young birds build relatively rudimentary ones,

What bowerbird bowers are for: A male Satin Bowerbird offers a visiting female one of his precious blue decorations.

and often either leave out the decorations altogether or bring the wrong ones. Female Satin Bowerbirds prefer bowers that are well made and beautifully decorated, especially if the decorations are unusual ones. Males steal decorations from one another, disrupt one another's courtships, or tear apart the bowers of subordinate birds, in a constant battle for the females' attention.

The amount of work involved in building and decorating a bower must be considerable. The bower of the Great Bowerbird may be made of four to five thousand twigs, seven hundred or more in each wall, decorated with more than twelve hundred stones. Over a twenty-square-foot (2 m²) area, a Great Bowerbird may assemble between five and twelve thousand objects, weighing in total as much as twenty-five pounds (11 kg).

The reward for having the best bower is substantial. Observers keeping track of twenty-two male Satin Bowerbirds in 1981 recorded 212 copulations. More than half of them—56 percent—were the work of just five of the male birds.

A female bowerbird chooses her mate carefully. When a female arrives to inspect a male Spotted Bowerbird's bower, it throws him into a frenzy of excited display. He runs in circles around or toward the bower walls, often stopping to throw his decorations about, pouring out a torrent of song that includes, according to the behavioral ecologist John Alcock, mimicry of other birds, hisses, clicks, and the sounds of barking dogs and twanging fence wires. Even with all this enthusiasm, she is more likely to leave than to stay and mate. Alcock notes:

> [A]lthough male bowerbirds have enjoyed fame as a result of their endeavors as architects, artists, and actors, their behavior probably is primarily the evolutionary product of female sales resistance. The cold-eyed scrutiny of generations of females has left males chained to their bowers, like housewives to their ironing boards.

It appears that bowerbirds started out as brightly colored birds, but gradually transferred the lures they held out to prospective mates from their feathers to their bowers. The male MacGregor's Bowerbird carries an immense orange brush sweeping from his crown that he erects and switches back and forth violently when a female approaches. His bower is less impressive than that of his shorter-crested cousin, the Streaked Bowerbird—whose bower in turn fades into insignificance when compared with the truly remarkable structure built by the Vogelkop Bowerbird, who has no crest at all. This bird, the dullest of the whole family, starts out building what looks like a typical maypole bower, but covers it with an arched roof that fooled early naturalists into thinking that the whole structure was a hut built for human children. The Vogelkop is the only maypole builder to paint his bower.

Among the avenue-building bowerbirds, the dazzling orange-red Flame Bowerbird of northern New Guinea builds a crude, simply decorated avenue of thin twigs. On the other hand, the most spectacular avenue bower, with four walls instead of the usual two, is built by the plain-looking Yellow-breasted Bowerbird of central New Guinea. The Yellow-breasted Bowerbird's behavior suggests that he once had bright colors, but has lost them. Several of this bowerbird's closest relatives sport a small but very bright purple crest on the backs of their heads. When they display to a female, they turn their heads, fanning their crests to show off their one bright patch of color. So does the Yellow-breasted—but he has no crest. The behavior has stayed on, even though the ornament it once displayed is gone; the bird now achieves the same end with the complicated structure of its bower.

Why should a shift like this have happened? Gerald Borgia, who has studied bowerbird evolution, points out that the Tooth-billed Bowerbird typically captures females that attend his court, often biting them behind the neck as he copulates. This sort of rough treatment may discourage some females from visiting at all. A bower, though, gives the female a place to hide. She usually keeps part of it between her and its urgently displaying owner, giving her a chance for a quick getaway if she decides not to mate. That degree of added insurance may make her more likely to visit males in the first place—and that, of course, is the point.

OUT IN THE FIELD

No field guide on earth can match the company of someone who already knows the birds and where to find them. If you are new at birding, the smartest thing you can do is either to go out with an experienced birder or to join a field trip led by a knowledgeable guide. Most museums and local natural-history societies run regular field-trip programs, and you should seriously consider going with one of them. Finding, and joining, your local natural history society or bird club is a good idea in any case.

Of course you are bound to feel a little frustrated. Your guide will identify birds so far away that you can barely tell they are birds at all, or will name birds by voice alone or spot birds that have disappeared by the time you have figured out where to look for them. If you have these experiences, it does not mean that birding is not for you. Every birder alive has had the same sort of growing pains, or for that matter still has them now and again. There is nothing magical about what your guide is doing. All you need to do the same thing is patience and experience.

If you want to get the most out of watching birds, you should learn what to expect, where to look, and which birds are likely to be around at different times of year. For example, if you see a shrike in the northern United States or southern Canada, it will almost certainly be a Loggerhead Shrike in spring or summer and a Northern Shrike in winter. It is extremely unusual for either bird to be around at the wrong time of year.

You don't need a lot of fancy equipment to go birding. Good binoculars, though, are a must. You can find a lot of advice, if you look, about which sort of binoculars to buy, but I think this is very much an individual choice. Bear in mind, though, that there is more to binoculars than magnifying power. A large and powerful set may seem like a good idea in the store, but can become a millstone around your neck on a long hike. Also, the more powerful the magnification on a pair of binoculars, the harder they will be to hold steady and the smaller your field of view will be when you look through them. This can make it quite difficult to get the bird that you can plainly see without your binoculars in your sights when you try to look through them. Today, high-powered binoculars are much more lightweight and easy to use than they were when I started birding, but it is still worthwhile, especially considering their price, to take your time in making a selection until you find some that feel right. For a beginning birder, seven- or eight-power binoculars, with a field of view of thirty-five degrees or more, are probably your best choice.

A telescope is also essential equipment for serious birders, but it is usually not much use in seeing songbirds. For larger birds such as ducks or shorebirds that hold still in the open at a long distance, a telescope may be very useful indeed.

One piece of equipment that many birders forget is a notebook. Keep a record of the birds you see, of their appearance and behavior, and when and where you saw them. You may also want to keep a "life list" of the birds you have seen—a very entertaining pursuit, but one that should not blind you to the fact that a new bird is more than a tick on your list, and an old bird is still worth looking at.

Finally, and most important, be an ethical birder. The golden rule applies to birding as it does to anything else, and the "others" that you do unto include the birds themselves, other wildlife, places, and people. The American Birding Association has developed a Code of Birding Ethics. I have included it at the back of this book, and it is one of the most important of the resources I have placed there. I hope that you will read it and follow it. Its two guiding principles are so important, though, that they are worth repeating here:

Everyone who enjoys birds and birding must always respect wildlife, its environment, and the rights of others.

In any conflict of interest between birds and birders, the welfare of the birds and their environment comes first.

FIVE

W H Y   S I N G ?

The nightingale does here make choice
To sing the trials of her voice.
Low shrubs she sits in, and adorns
With music high the squatted thorns.
But highest oaks stoop down to hear,
And listening elders prick the ear.
The thorn, lest it should hurt her, draws
Within the skin its shrunken claws.

—ANDREW MARVELL, *UPON APPLETON HOUSE*

A Song Sparrow cannot learn the song of its close relative the Swamp Sparrow, and vice versa.

Long before Marvell, and for long after, poets, playwrights, and musicians have found inspiration and solace in the songs of birds. Filtered through an artist's imagination, songbirds sing to us from the pages of Keats or Shelley, or from the stage in Wagner's *Siegfried* or Stravinsky's *The Nightingale.*

Bird songs, transcribed, decorate Vivaldi's *The Four Seasons*, Beethoven's *Pastoral* Symphony, or the prelude to Richard Strauss' *Der Rosenkavalier*. The singing birds themselves are evoked in pieces like Vaughan Williams' *The Lark Ascending*. The deeply religious twentieth-century French composer-naturalist Olivier Messiaen used the songs of more than three hundred species of birds from around the world, sometimes vastly transmogrified or inflated, as the chief building blocks for huge, mystical tapestries of orchestral, organ, and piano music with titles such as *Oiseaux exotiques*, *Catalogue d'oiseaux*, *Chronochromie*, or *Couleurs de la cité céleste.*

Bird songs fill the soundtracks of movies, often with little verisimilitude: the Screaming Piha of the Amazon can be heard in the movie *Jurassic Park*, which is supposed to be taking place

Like many of the world's great songbird vocalists, the Nightingale, inspiration of poets and composers, is a plain creature.

off Costa Rica (the dinosaurs themselves, by the way, scream with the voices of, among other things, geese, egrets, and—for the awesome *Tyrannosaurus rex*—penguins).

Birds have told us, in more than one language, what names to call them: currawong, eechong, uguisu, chiffchaff, phoebe, pewee. The bellbird's clang and the catbird's mew are echoed in their names, whether the name "bellbird" is applied to a South American cotinga or an Australasian honeyeater, or whether the name "catbird" is attached to a thickset green bowerbird from eastern Australia or a slim gray relative of mockingbirds and thrashers in North America.

Songbirds produce a tremendous range of sounds, some beautiful (at least to us), some—like the toy-bugle tootling of the Trumpeter Finch or the ululating wail of the Wallcreeper—quite startling. The reactions they provoke in us can vary from joy to irritation. The great Edwardian naturalist W. H. Hudson, who grew up in Argentina, rhapsodized about the song of the White-banded Mockingbird:

For my part I can think of no other way to describe the surpassing excellence of its melody, which delights the soul beyond all other bird-music, than by saying that this bird is among song-birds like the diamond among stones, which in its many-coloured splendour represents and exceeds the special beauty of every other gem.

On the other hand, he found the incessantly repeated two-syllabled call of the Pale-breasted Spinetail "quite as distressing as the grating song of a cicada."

Songbirds can produce sounds of great harmonic complexity—but complexity may not equal beauty. A White-throated Sparrow haunts the traveler in the Canadian North with only two whistled pitches, while the Brown-headed Cowbird, whose harsh *glug-glug-glee* covers four octaves (the greatest known frequency range in the songs of any bird) in a second or two, has yet to inspire a poet.

Songbirds, though, do not sing for us—not even for the poets, musicians, and naturalists among us. They sing for themselves, and it is the purpose of this chapter to ask why. There are several answers, but whatever they are, human aesthetics is not among them. Voice is a tool, or even a weapon, that helps songbirds to survive and reproduce.

Before looking at *why* birds sing, we ought to consider *how*. You will remember that birds do not make sounds with their larynx, as we do, but with a special organ called the syrinx. Comparing our larynx to the syrinx of a songbird, in fact, is like comparing a tin whistle to a symphony orchestra.

The syrinx is part of a breathing apparatus far more efficient than our own. Bird lungs are connected to a series of air sacs that fill much of their bodies. When a bird inhales, air passes right through the lungs into a *posterior air sac*. It is not until the bird exhales that the air actually passes through the tiny tubules in the lung where oxygen is extracted. Even then, the air does not escape the bird's body, but is sent forward into an *anterior air sac*. It is not until the next breathing cycle that the air finally is exhaled. With this system, a bird can keep air flowing continuously through its lungs. This efficiency does not just make for better breathing, but for better control of song. The syrinx structure works so well that almost all the air that passes through it makes sound, compared with our lowly 2 percent.

Our larynx sounds when the air we exhale vibrates our vocal cords. A bird's syrinx has no vocal cords. Instead, it produces sound by vibrating membranes in its walls. An air sac, the *interclavicular*, surrounds the syrinx, bringing pressure to the outside of the membranes. We know that this is absolutely necessary for the bird to sing, because if you puncture the air sac, the bird becomes voiceless until the wound heals. The combination of air pressure from the sac on the outside and pressure from the exhaling air on the inside sets the membranes vibrating.

Syringeal muscles control the tension of the membranes, which in turn controls the frequency of the sound. The singer opens its beak and flutters its throat, manipulating the sounds as they emerge, as we do with our lips and tongue. To make things even more complicated, each side of the syrinx operates independently. A songbird literally sings duets with itself, combining the different sounds from the right and left halves of the syrinx to produce the song we hear.

But why do bird songs sound the way they do? Why do the haunting tones of the Slate-colored Solitaire sound from the cloud forest, and the totally different, joyous jumble of the Skylark from high over an open field? It is not just that these birds are unrelated—the solitaire is a thrush and the Skylark is a lark—though related birds may well sing similar songs. It is because of *where* they sing.

The biggest physical difference between bird sounds separates pure clear whistles (like the song of the solitaire) from highly modulated noises that may be filled with harmonics (like the Skylark's trill). Harmonics change the quality of sound, from a chirp to a buzz to a rattle. They are the reason a violin does not sound like a flute, even when you play the same note on both.

Eugene Morton wanted to know if the kind of sound a bird makes had anything to do with the kind of habitat it lives in. To find out, he used mechanical sound generators to record both pure whistles and random, highly modulated noise. He played his artificial bird songs in forests, grasslands, and other habitats in Panama, and tested how well the different types of sounds carried to microphones hung at various heights and distances.

He found that the physical attributes of a habitat affect the way sound carries. Pure whistled tones carry better in forests than in open grassland, because pure whistles are distorted by the air turbulence on a windy plain or by the currents set up when open ground heats in the sun. Highly modulated sounds carry better in open country than in forests, where they are muffled by echoes as the sounds bounce off tree trunks and the canopy.

When Morton turned to the birds themselves, he found that the types of songs his mechanical experiments predicted would carry best in each habitat are, generally speaking, the sounds that the birds living there actually make. Antbirds, thrushes, warblers, and other birds of the forest depths sing with long, pure whistles. Sparrows and larks in open country sing complex, jumbled, harmonic songs. Closely related birds sing the type of song you would expect from their habitat, not from their relationships. The Tawny-crowned Greenlet, a tropical vireo of the forest understory, sings a long, low whistle, while the Scrub Greenlet, which lives in shrubby open country, has a completely different, modulated song.

Bird songs not only have to carry in a habitat, but must compete with other noises. Birds that live along rushing streams often have high-pitched, piercing calls that are easy to hear against the noise of the torrent.

A high perch may help sound to carry farther, and many songbirds sing from the highest perch they can find. In grasslands there are no high perches available, so birds may fly high into the air, instead, and hover there, singing—a behavior called *skylarking* after the European Skylark, but you can hear Sprague's Pipits and McCown's Longspurs do it in North American grasslands, or Brown Songlarks (which are not larks) on the plains of Australia.

Even the timing of song may relate to its carrying power. There is usually less wind at dawn, and so bird songs will carry farther in the stiller air. Perhaps as a result, the coming of day is heralded by a dawn chorus. The half light of daybreak may be too dim for a bird to hunt for food—another of several possible reasons for a songbird to spend its waking time singing.

Birders, and most bird guides, usually divide the sounds that songbirds make into two categories: songs and calls. One definition offered by Clive Catchpole and Peter Slater in their book *Bird Song*, says that "songs tend to be long, complex, vocalizations produced by males in the breeding season" and "calls tend to be shorter, simpler and produced by both sexes throughout the year." Some bird songs, though, are quite unimpressive. Henslow's Sparrow, despite great puffing of its feathers and tossing of its head, can produce no more than a faint, almost inaudible *slick*. The division has less to do with what a sound is like than with what it is for. The sounds a bird makes are almost all for communication; the difference lies in what is being communicated, and to whom.

Song tells females that a mate is available, and other males that the singer is in possession of his territory and will brook no challenge. It is a message that must be repeated over and over, for as long as the bird needs to get it across. Once a male Great Tit or Marsh Warbler has won his mate, he may sing less often; a Reed Bunting switches to a different song type. When a Sedge Warbler pairs, he stops singing altogether—but Great Tits cannot do that. If their song stops, even for a day, rivals may move in. When singing male Great Tits were removed from their territories, other tits took over the unclaimed land within ten hours. However, if the scientists who removed the birds played recordings of their songs within their territories, it took more than thirty daylight hours before a new owner took possession.

Calls are used for everything else: to sound alarms, to let parent birds know their chicks want to be fed, to make mating noises, and to keep a flock together. Black-capped Chickadees use a special *squawk* to stimulate their nestlings to gape for food. Chickadees, indeed, take their name from a call; their songs are far less memorable.

Bird guides—which have to simplify things—may describe "the" song of a songbird, as though each species had only one. For some birds, this is true. An Ovenbird generally has only one song—a ringing crescendo: *teach-er teach-ER TEACH-ER!*—though he may sing a more varied "extended" song, especially at twilight. Many birds, however, can ring a great variety of subtle changes on their basic song pattern, using a vocabulary of musical syllables to build up a *song repertoire*. Repertoire size makes a difference: Western Meadowlarks with larger repertoires have greater success in finding a mate, and greater breeding success once they do.

Some Brown-headed Cowbird songs get a stronger response from a female than others. Any male cowbird can sing these "high potency" songs, but only the dominant males usually do. These songs are their particular property, and they will attack any subordinate male that dares to sing them within their hearing.

The number of songs in a songbird's repertoire varies enormously from species to species. A single male Northern Cardinal can sing eight to twelve songs, a Sedge Wren more than a hundred, a Nightingale from one to three hundred, and a Brown Thrasher at least two thousand. A European Sedge Warbler has a vocabulary of only fifty or so song syllables, but he can string them together, like the dots and dashes of Morse code, in so many ways that he may never repeat the same full song twice in his life.

Song variants may convey different messages. Five-striped Sparrows and Great Reed Warblers use longer songs to attract females and shorter songs to repel rival males. If a Cetti's Warbler finds another male invading his territory, he switches to a song he saves especially for close, aggressive encounters. The Chestnut-sided Warbler, like many other wood warblers, sings two categories of song. Accented songs, ending in an explosive crack ("*I want to see Miss BEECH-er!*"), seem to be most important for signaling to females. They vary little, and their role may simply be to proclaim that a mate is available. Unaccented songs, which vary much more, are used for close encounters with rival males, where it may be important for the warbler to signal not just his presence but his precise, changing mood.

Songbirds may need a prodigious memory to store their repertoire of songs. Winter Wrens in Oregon sing about thirty different songs, each one lasting eight seconds and consisting of as many as fifty notes. Marsh Wrens and Northern Cardinals switch from song to song in a predictable way, so they have to remember both the songs and the order in which to sing them—though whether this requires extra memory processing, we cannot say.

Female birds react to the serenades of their males at a hormonal level. If you play the song of a Canary to a caged female, you may stimulate her to build a nest or lay an egg. If you play her a larger repertoire, she will build her nest faster, lay eggs sooner, and, astonishingly enough, even lay larger clutches. Yellowhammers and Northern Mockingbirds sing more when they are about to nest. Their songs might actually stimulate the female's reproductive cycle, or possibly chase off rivals trying to sneak a quick pairing when their mates are most fertile. Female European Starlings

One of the typical
sounds of the forests
of eastern Australia is
the duet of a pair of
Eastern Whipbirds,
particularly the ring-
ing whipcrack of the
male.

and Pied Flycatchers checking out nest boxes were more likely to visit a box if it was fitted with a loudspeaker playing male song. When female Dunnocks are in their fertile period, they respond to the songs of male Dunnocks; moreover, they prefer their own mate's, showing that not only are they attracted to male song, but they can tell one male from another.

A male Red-winged Blackbird, but not a female, can be fooled by a Northern Mockingbird imitating his song. This does not mean that females are smarter than males, but it does mean that they are more discriminating. A female Red-wing may run little risk of mating with a mockingbird, but while a male that makes a mistake may only waste some time, a female that cannot tell one male from another may end up with an inappropriate father for her young.

These sorts of findings show two things. One is that song is important when it comes to attracting a female. The other is that any old song won't do; females have their preferences. Great Reed Warbler females in Sweden, for example, check out several singing males before deciding on a mate. They prefer males that sing longer songs, and males with more songs in their repertoire frequently cuckold their less talented neighbors.

Some female birds sing, too. Females of at least nine North American wood warblers will sing on rare occasions. Female Red-winged Blackbirds have two types of song: one that they use to answer their mates and another that is a challenge to rival females. The most interesting female songs, though, may be the ones they sing with their mates, in chorus or duet.

Far from being the land of "songless bright birds," Australia may be the land of avian choral societies. The caroling of a communal group of Australian Magpies, males and females joining together in chorus to defend their territory, is as typical a sound of Australia as the Kookaburra's laugh. The incessant tinkling of a colony of Bell Miners, or the raucous cackling of a group of Chowchillas, are equally evocative, respectively, of the eucalypt woodlands of the Southeast and the rainforests of the North.

In eastern Australian forests, the drawn-out *eeeeee-WHIP!* of the male Eastern Whipbird is answered by a sharp *chew-chew* from the female. A pair of Rufous-breasted Wrens in Venezuela alternate phrases with such split-second timing that the whole thing sounds like the outpouring of a single bird. A female Black-headed Gonolek, an African bush-shrike, answers the cry of her mate after only 144 milliseconds, a response time humans cannot match.

More than two hundred species of birds in forty-four families are known to sing duets. North American birders may not realize how widespread duetting is, because most of the birds that duet live in the Tropics. Here, a pair of birds may patrol their territory year-round. If they live in dense undergrowth or shrubbery, singing duets may be the best way they have of keeping in touch.

Duetting may be a way for each singer to check up on his or her mate's activities. A bird that is busy synchronizing duets cannot be off committing adultery with a neighbor. It has been suggested that the duets of the Slate-colored Boubou developed as each bird tried to keep the other from singing by itself, an activity that could bring in a sexual rival. If this theory is correct, duets may be not so much a cooperative effort as an audible example of the battle of the sexes.

With song playing such an important part in songbird lives, it is crucial that the birds grow up able to perform, and recognize, their own species' vocal repertoire to the best of their ability.

Suboscine birds hatch with their vocal repertoires hard-wired into their brains, though the bellbirds require months of practice to perfect their *bock* calls. The oscines—the true songbirds—have to learn their songs, the only birds, other than parrots and hummingbirds, to do so. Even an oscine, though, is born with some ability to recognize its own kind. When young Song Sparrows heard the song of their own species for the first time, their hearts actually beat faster—but this did not happen if they were played the song of a different species. Certainly, these birds had never had a chance to learn the difference. They must have hatched already knowing it.

The most important—and, for many species, the only—time in a songbird's life for song learning is in its first year. Song Sparrows, Swamp Sparrows, and Nightingales do most, if not all, of their song learning early in life. Some birds, including Canaries, Village Indigobirds, and at least some Yellow Warblers and American Redstarts, can keep learning in later years. So, as we shall see, can such mimics as the Northern Mockingbird. Young male Indigo Buntings do not learn the songs of their fathers, but copy the song of an older male neighbor on their return from their first journey to the Tropics. Once they have settled on a song, they sing it for the rest of their lives.

A Chaffinch can learn songs only until it is about ten to twelve months old and its testosterone levels rise for the first time. What would happen if a Chaffinch went through its first year of life without hearing the song of an adult? To find out, W. H. Thorpe, a pioneer in birdsong research, raised young Chaffinches in isolation cages, cut off from the songs of their own species. The isolated birds did sing, but their song was much less complex and musical

Male Indigo Buntings copy the song of an older neighbor, and sing it for the rest of their lives.

than their species' normal song. It seems that there are actually two aspects to a Chaffinch song. One is inherited, giving only the basic outline of the full vocalization. To fill in the rest, the bird must learn.

It turns out that nature has tried Thorpe's experiment. On the high peaks of the islands of Tenerife and Gran Canaria in the Canary Islands lives a second species of chaffinch. The Blue Chaffinch is larger and, as you might expect, bluer than its mainland cousins. It is also bluer than the rather distinctive Canary Island forms of the ordinary Chaffinch that live farther down the slopes of the same mountains.

While in the Canaries in 1976 I made a very poor tape recording of a singing male Blue Chaffinch. Dr. Luis Baptista, an expert on song learning, later told me that my recording sounded like the song of an ordinary Chaffinch raised in isolation. The Canaries had acted like a giant isolation laboratory. Remote from others of their species, the first chaffinches to arrive there—the ancestors of the Blue Chaffinch—had forgotten how to sing.

What is it, exactly, that the birds are learning? Not, it seems, simply a tune. Instead, birds react to specific elements in the songs they hear. These may be changes in frequency, pattern, or lengths of song phrases. The phrases don't even have to be in order. Indigo Buntings recognized phrases of Indigo Bunting songs even when the phrases were played back in the wrong sequence or at the wrong pitch.

White-throated Sparrows respond to the regular pattern and the pitch of their species' song. Brown Thrashers sound rather like their cousin the Gray Catbird, except that thrashers repeat each phrase before going on to the next one. A thrasher apparently recognizes its own song by listening for the repetitions. If there are none, then the other singer is probably a catbird and the thrasher can go about its business unconcerned.

Most songbirds grow up hearing the songs of many different kinds of birds. How do they avoid learning the wrong song? Sometimes, it seems, they could not learn the song of the wrong species if they tried. A Swamp Sparrow makes a simple trill of rapidly repeated notes on one pitch, while a Song Sparrow has a much more complicated and varied song, usually starting with two or three buzzes on the same pitch, followed by a jumble of other notes. Song Sparrows apparently cannot learn Swamp Sparrow songs, and Swamp Sparrows cannot learn Song Sparrow songs, because their learning processes are different. Swamp Sparrows learn their songs by focusing on the timing of the repeated notes of their trill, and Song Sparrows simply can't do that. On the other hand, Swamp Sparrows cannot learn the varied syllables that make up the song of a Song Sparrow.

Nature isn't perfect, however, and sometimes birds do learn the wrong song. Luis Baptista

(opposite) **The Blue Chaffinch, descendant of ordinary chaffinches that arrived in the Canary Islands in the distant past, is found only on high elevations of Gran Canaria and Tenerife. Its song is much simpler than that of its continental cousin.**

has found that a captive White-crowned Sparrow will not learn the song of a Red Avadavat from a tape recording, but that it can learn it from a live avadavat—not something that is ever likely to happen in nature, of course, since the two species live on different continents. At Point Pelee in southern Ontario, I once heard a Carolina Wren sing the song of a House Wren. It was quite a performance, because the Carolina Wren has a much larger and more ringing voice than a House Wren. Carolina Wrens are fairly rare at Pelee, but House Wrens are common. Perhaps the Carolina had been hearing too much of the wrong song.

African indigobirds, by contrast, learn nothing but "wrong" songs. Instead of building a nest, each species lays its eggs in the nest of a single, related species of finch. The young birds grow up learning the song of their host, either from the hosts themselves or from adults of their own species. While Red-billed Firefinches sing one song each, the Village Indigobirds that grow up in their nests keep three firefinch songs in their repertoire, picking them up from other indigobirds. This may give them a better chance of luring in a female with a song that sounds, to her, like her foster father.

Many birds—White-throated Sparrows, Song Sparrows, European Robins, Hooded Warblers, and more—can recognize the songs of their neighbors. They react much more strongly to the song of a stranger—who might be trying to invade their territory—than to the bird next door defending its own plot of land. Furthermore, since songbirds learn their songs by listening to other members of their own species, they tend to sound like the other birds they hear. Corn Buntings in Europe and Village Indigobirds in Africa seem to learn their whole repertoires from nearby birds. Over time, a local accent, or *song dialect*, can develop. The songs of Chowchillas, Carolina Wrens, Bewick's Wrens, White-crowned Sparrows, and many others change from place to place. On the central coast of California—but not in Alaska—White-crowned Sparrow dialects may change sharply every few miles. Not only do dialects differ from place to place, but, like human speech patterns, they may change over time. Robert Payne found that Indigo Bunting dialects usually lasted no more than fifteen years, the equivalent of three bunting generations. White-crowned and Rufous-collared Sparrow dialects may last more than twenty years—but the distinctive songs a colony of Yellow-rumped Caciques sings may not last out a single breeding season.

Why learn at all? We don't really know. The need to learn may just be something that happened to the oscines early in their evolution, and that they cannot now escape. But the more we know about the variety of oscine song, the more it seems that the flexibility of song learning gives birds a real social, and perhaps environmental, advantage as they jostle for space or stake out new habitats. Consider, for example, the song duels Marsh Wrens fight over their territories.

Marsh Wren duels have actually affected the brain structure of the participants. To be a successful duelist, a bird needs a large repertoire of songs—the larger the better—and that means an enhanced brain capable of managing and remembering all the elements that make up a champion's arsenal.

Songbirds have a special area, a *high vocal center*, in the corpus luteum of their forebrains, that is devoted to song learning. It contains special song-control nuclei, part of a distinct neural pathway connecting the brain and the syrinx. The size of the center, and the number of song-control nuclei that it contains, is not static. Birds with more songs in their repertoire have larger song-control nuclei.

Marsh Wrens are found all across North America, but Marsh Wrens in California face tougher competition than wrens in the East. That competition has driven them to expand their repertoires to around 150 songs, three times the size of those their cousins sing in the marshes of New York State—and California birds have a 40 percent larger volume of song-control nuclei than do New York birds. This brain difference really does mean a difference in a Marsh Wren's learning ability. Captive California birds learned more than twice as many songs as birds from New York. In the battle for Marsh Wren territory, brains and talent win the day.

The ultimate development of song learning is mimicry. Mimics learn not only their own songs, but the songs of other birds or the calls of other animals. Some even pick up mechan-

Male Marsh Wrens
from California have
much larger song
repertoires than
Marsh Wrens from
New York state. Song
duels among western
Marsh Wrens have
even affected the
structure of their
brains.

ical noises. A Northern Mockingbird can learn new sounds throughout its life. The result is one of the most complicated and extensive library of whistles, buzzes, and chirps packed into the brain of any bird. A male mockingbird may have more than 150 songs at his disposal.

Mockingbirds are famous mimics. So are the Old World starlings and mynas, which may be the mockingbirds' closest cousins. So are some of the most celebrated songsters in the world: Australian lyrebirds and scrub-birds, African robin-chats, and Lawrence's Thrush of South America, a bird whose song appears to consist of nothing but imitations of other birds, arranged into a seemingly endless collage.

The European Marsh Warbler picks up the songs of dozens of African birds on its wintering ground and sings them on its breeding grounds in Europe. Bowerbirds—as if their building abilities were not enough—are accomplished mimics. A Tooth-billed Bowerbird's imitations of White-throated Treecreepers and others even hold up under audiospectographic analysis.

The Superb Lyrebird imitates at least fifteen different species of birds. It is an astonishing experience—one I have had the good fortune to enjoy—to watch a dancing lyrebird and hear issuing from beneath its tail the sounds of a duetting pair of Eastern Whipbirds, two kookaburras singing at what seems to be the same time, or a whole flock of parrots chattering in concert. Strangely, though lyrebirds mimic many of the species of birds that share their habitat, they will not imitate a bird that breeds at the same time as they do. Thus, one of the most commonly imitated birds in the southern part of the Superb's range, the Eastern Whipbird, is not imitated farther north where whipbirds sing during the lyrebirds' winter breeding season. This may be to avoid confusion; a male lyrebird is interested in attracting female lyrebirds, not whipbirds.

Though many songbirds can learn songs only in their first few months of life, this young Northern Mockingbird will continue to add new sounds to his repertoire as long as he lives.

The most spectacular and accomplished mimic in the bird world may be the Superb Lyrebird. No other bird combines a virtuoso vocal performance with such a dazzling display.

Mimicry is certainly impressive, but what is it for? We are still not exactly sure. There may be more than one answer. Mimicry may allow a bird to challenge birds of other species and keep them out of its territory. When its nest is threatened, the Thick-billed Euphonia, a small tanager from Central America, calls for reinforcements by imitating the calls other birds use when they mob a predator.

Male Northern Mockingbirds direct most of their mimicry at potential mates. If a larger vocal repertoire increases a male's chance of getting a mate, imitating the songs of other birds may be a cheap and effective way of outsinging a rival. Perhaps the bowerbirds, who borrow or steal physical objects from their surroundings to decorate their bowers, are doing the same thing in a musical way when they appropriate the songs of the birds they hear around them.

This explanation won't work for the most famous songbird mimic of all, the Hill Myna. Hill Mynas have been prized as pets because of their uncanny ability to imitate human speech—a gift that has seen them heavily trapped for the pet trade. Hill Mynas—like the most famous non-songbird mimics, the parrots—do not seem to sing at all. Their ability to mimic may be a byproduct of their social life. Hill Mynas live in groups that share their calls with one another. Because their calls vary tremendously, they have to be good at copying each other's calls, and that skill may, perhaps by evolutionary accident, give them the ability that has landed so many behind the bars of a cage.

USING YOUR EARS

One of my first jobs, as an undergraduate zoology student in the 1960s, was as field assistant to Dr. J. Murray Speirs. I could not have done better. For summer after summer, Dr. Speirs taught me to identify birds not just by sight but by sound. This skill was absolutely necessary for our work. Only by knowing the songs and calls of forest birds could we get a real idea of just how many there were in our study areas. I still cannot match the keenness of Dr. Speirs' ear, but what he taught me opened a world of ornithological experience. You may not be as fortunate in your teacher as I was, but even so, learning to recognize birds by voice can open the same world for you.

We have long known that each species of bird may sing its own song. Gilbert White, the careful and enthusiastic naturalist of Selborne, listened attentively to the "little yellow bird…[that] still continues to make a sibulous shivering noise in the tops of tall woods" and, by 1768, announced that "I have now, past dispute, made out three distinct species of the willow-wrens (*motacillae trochili*) which constantly and invariably use distinct notes." Today, English birders call them the Wood Warbler, the Willow Warbler, and the Chiffchaff.

Song can be the best way to identify birds such as sparrows, warblers, and flycatchers. You cannot learn bird songs, though, by reading their descriptions in your field guide. Short of actual experience with someone who knows, the only way to learn bird songs is to listen to recordings, on tape, compact disc, or CD-ROM. There are a good many choices available, including tapes and discs designed to accompany the Peterson and *National Geographic* guides. They repay close listening and study. Be aware, though, that most of these tapes give only the commonest or most typical songs and calls. The birds you actually hear in the field may not sound like the ones on the recording (any more than they will look exactly like the pictures in your field guide). To hear a wider range of calls for each species, you will need more detailed tapes devoted to specific songbird families. Cornell University publishes an excellent one on warblers.

Everybody agrees that tapes and tape recorders are wonderful tools for learning bird songs before you go into the field, or for refreshing your memory when you are there. However, no subject in birding arouses more vehement arguments than the use of tapes to lure shy or skulking birds into the open. The easiest way to see some shy birds well is to challenge them with the taped song of their own species. That's all very well as far as the birder is concerned, but what about the bird? Every time a bird responds to a tape, it is wasting energy that could be spent finding food, caring for its young, or dealing with real challenges to its territorial supremacy. It is possible that enough disturbances of this sort, or the wrong ones at the wrong time, could make the difference between whether a bird succeeds in rearing its brood or not. So should tapes be used?

If you are in an area that gets a lot of disturbance, particularly from birders, or are chasing a rare bird that has been disturbed over and over again by people trying to see it, you should not use a tape. In some cases it might even be illegal. In the United States, using a tape to lure a bird such as Kirtland's Warbler could violate the Endangered Species Act. National parks and reserves in Florida, such as the Everglades, have banned the use of tapes to lure birds. On the other hand, the occasional, judicious use of tapes may be no more disturbing than any other activity. As for so many other things, you should use moderation.

If you are tired of using other people's recordings, you can make your own. You can record bird songs with almost any portable tape recorder, but to get recordings of decent quality you need a machine with a good frequency response and, in particular, a good directional microphone or a microphone mounted in a parabolic reflector. Always be sure to make careful notes, preferably on the tape, on where and when you made your recordings, the identity of the singer (it's easy to forget later!), and what it was doing at the time.

High-quality recordings are more than just birding tools. They can be valuable scientific documents. If you make any really unusual ones, consider donating copies to the Library of Recorded Sound at the Cornell Laboratory of Ornithology. Their address is 159 Sapsucker Woods Road, Ithaca, New York, U.S.A. 14850 (e-mail: libnatsounds@cornell.edu).

SIX

FAMILY VALUES

'Tis spring, warm glows the south,
Chaffinch carries the Moss in his mouth
To filbert hedges all day long,
And charms the poet with his beautiful song;
The wind blows bleak o'er the sedgy fen,
But warm the sun shines by the little wood,
Where the old cow at her leisure chews her cud.

—JOHN CLARE, *BIRD'S NESTS*

A family group of Superb Fairy-Wrens may include a brightly colored male, young males, and females. All members of the group help to rear the breeding pair's young.

The payoff for a songbird's investment in territory, display, song, and mate choice comes at nesting time. To make that payoff mean something, the young she produces must be given every chance to survive. Nesting is a risky business, and the failure rate can be high. Nest predators are the greatest threat breeding songbirds face, but eggs and young are also at risk from exposure and, once they hatch, starvation.

How good a chance a brood has depends on choices their parents make even before they begin to build a nest—choices such as when to build and where. Male Australian grass finches lead their mates from potential site to potential site, sometimes inspecting as many as a hundred possibilities before the female finally accepts one. Though in the Tropics birds like the Barred Antshrike may nest in any month of the year, temperate songbirds must time their nesting to make sure their young hatch when food is most abundant.

American Robins begin nesting when the humidity reaches about 50 percent and the temperature averages between forty-five and sixty-five degrees Fahrenheit (7–18°C). Birds that depend on irregular food supplies have to be more flexible. Red Crossbills, for example, can take

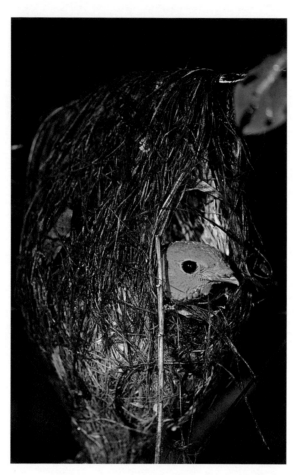

Like many rainforest birds, the Green Broadbill of Southeast Asia builds a covered nest that may be more difficult for such predators as snakes to reach.

advantage of an abundant autumn seed crop among Rocky Mountain conifers by nesting in the winter. Dry-country birds may have to wait for sporadic rains before starting to breed. Zebra Finches in Australia breed about four months after the rains, when they can supply their young with ripening grass seeds.

Where to build can depend on details of climate. Pinyon Jays prefer the south side of a pine tree, which may be thirty-five to thirty-seven degrees Fahrenheit (2 to 3°C) warmer than the north. Spiderhunters in Southeast Asia attach their nest to the underside of a large leaf, where it is sheltered from tropical rains. To avoid overheating, Desert Larks in Israel choose a north-facing site sheltered by a bush or a stone. A Cactus Wren's nest in a bush or cholla cactus must be protected from cold winds early in the season, and from the desert's heat later on. In the same American deserts, Verdins often raise their first brood in an east-facing nest warmed by the morning sun, then switch to one facing southwest for a second brood.

Climate can affect a nest's structure as well as its placement. Helmeted Honeyeaters build bulkier nests in cold weather. An American Robin will use more flexible rootlets to build its nest if the site it has chosen is particularly windy, and will add extra moss to the lining if it is particularly cold. The more insulation there is in a Village Weaver nest, the less time the female must spend sitting on her eggs.

The Cactus Wren of
the American
Southwest often nests
in a prickly cholla
cactus. Its choice is
probably to deter
predators, but where
it puts the nest within
the cholla may be
determined by the
heat of the sun.

The communal nest of a colony of Social Weavers looks something like a haystack in a tree. The nests are on the underside of the stack, protected from extremes of climate by the mound of material above them.

The most thoroughly insulated nest on earth belongs to the Social Weaver of southwestern Africa. Social Weavers work together to construct an enormous colonial nest, often several feet (1–2 m) thick, like a haystack pitchforked into a tree. Individual nest cavities are on the underside of the haystack. The bulk above them protects eggs and young from the extremes of desert climate. Cool in the daytime, its interior, warmed by heat soaked up during the day and by the bodies of the nesting birds, can be sixty-five to seventy-five degrees Fahrenheit (18 to 23 °C) warmer than the cold night air. Generations of Social Weavers may use the same nest; some are known to be more than a hundred years old.

The materials songbirds use to build their nests range from the bits of moss and cobweb collected by the European Penduline-Tit to coarse sticks, preferred by the Firewood-Gatherer, that are so large the builder can scarcely fly away with them. Long-tailed Tits and Goldcrests build their nests out of mosses, lichens, and cobwebs, and line them with more than two thousand feathers.

Nests may contain some odd decorations. A Pale-breasted Spinetail or a Great Crested Flycatcher may include scraps of shed snake or lizard skin. In South Africa, the Black-eared Finch-Lark decorates the edge of its nest with the scarlet lids of the burrows of a particular species of trapdoor spider. European Starlings twine yarrow into their nests—not for decoration, but for protection. Yarrow gives off chemicals that keep down the growth of bacteria, and may kill the eggs of lice that could drain more than 20 percent of a chick's blood.

Many of the decorations birds add to their nests make them hard to see, or at least to recognize. Blue-gray Gnatcatchers, Yellow-bellied Elaenias, and Chaffinches plaster lichens on the

outside of the nest. Varied Sittellas use bits of bark. The Bearded Greenbul of Africa works a living fern into its nest rim that stays green until after the young hatch.

Camouflage is not the only way for a nesting songbird to foil predators. The White-headed Buffalo Weaver adds an extra wall of defense by placing thorny twigs along the boughs leading to its nest, over a distance of several feet or more. Many tropical songbirds get free guard service by nesting near colonies of ants, bees, or wasps. House Sparrows and European Starlings may build on the edge of an eagle's eyrie, or even within the huge bulk of an osprey's nest. Red-bellied Malimbes, whose nests may be raided by monkeys, sometimes nest in colonies in the same tree as the largest monkey-eating hawk in central Africa, the Crowned Hawk-Eagle.

Many songbirds, but hardly any other birds, build roofed or domed nests. A covered nest, or a hanging pouch such as the superbly constructed nests of New World orioles and Old World weavers, may be harder for a predator like a snake to reach. There are a lot more snakes, particularly in trees, in the Tropics than in the Temperate Zone, and though only 6 percent of eastern North American songbirds build covered nests, 38 percent do in West Africa and 46 percent in Borneo. Even without snakes or other predators to deal with, a covered nest is better at keeping the nestlings dry, or in open country at protecting them from the sun. That is probably the reason most Galápagos

The Varied Sittella of Australia disguises its nest by plastering the outside with bits of bark and lichen, held in place with cobwebs.

The large dark opening this **Cape Penduline-Tit** seems about to enter is not really the entrance to its nest, but rather a convincing decoy. The actual entrance is through the crescent-shaped slit just above it, which the bird can close, as here, to increase the illusion.

finches build covered nests, though there is only one species of snake in the Galápagos.

The Cape Penduline-Tit makes a soft pouch of wool, cobwebs, and plant fibers, with a side entrance. The entrance is lined with sticky cobwebs, and the bird can close it when it is inside. Below the true entrance is a deep pocket that looks remarkably like the real way into the nest. When the true entrance is closed, the results might fool any predator into missing the genuine nest cavity.

Although many songbird nests are the work of both male and female, those of most finches, wood warblers, and orioles—both New and Old World varieties—are built by the female alone. Male Willow Flycatchers and Indigo Buntings may fly about with their mates as they build, but do not help. Their main interest may be to guard her from other males.

The nests songbirds build vary almost as much as the birds themselves. Songbirds may nest on the ground, in a tree, or even, like cocks-of-the-rock and the peculiar West African rock-fowl, on the face of a cliff. Nests in trees may sit on a branch or be suspended from a fork. Asian tailorbirds and African camaropteras stitch two or three large leaves together with cobwebs, making a pouch to hold their nest.

Swallows actually vary more in nesting habits than they do in appearance. Colonies of Bank Swallows tunnel six feet (2 m) into the face of a sandbank. Tree Swallows select a hole in a hollow tree. Many build nests of mud, either the open cups of the Barn Swallow or the bottlenecked gourds of the various species of cliff swallows.

The Black-and-Red Broadbill of Southeast Asia hangs a heavy, shapeless mass of twigs and debris from a thin branch suspended over a river. Even a predator that could recognize it for

A North American Cliff Swallow gathers mud for its bottle-shaped nest.

what it is would have quite a job getting out to it. In the New World Tropics, the Sulfur-rumped Flycatcher does not even bother to add a nest cavity to its collection of materials until the whole structure is assembled. Then it forces its way into the mass through the center and expands the nest cavity from the inside out.

The largest nests built by any pair of songbirds working alone belong to a group of oven-birds, the cacholotes. The nest of a pair of Brown Cacholotes—birds the size of a Blue Jay—may be more than four feet (1 m) long and twenty-eight inches (70 cm) high, with an entrance tube extending horizontally for another yard. The sticks the birds use to build it may be twenty inch-es (50 cm) long and as thick as your little finger. W. H. Hudson reported that he stood on the nest of a White-throated Cacholote "and stamped on it with my heavy boots without injuring it in the least." The birds use these massive structures only briefly, for breeding or sleeping—possibly as a way of avoiding parasites that could build up in an older nest. One pair of Brown Cacholotes built

The American orioles and their relatives are the New World nest-building equivalents of the weavers. Like many weavers, these displaying male Yellow-rumped Caciques nest in colonies.

seventeen in thirty-six months, an average of one enormous nest every sixty-two days.

Cacholotes are solitary, but some songbirds—many swallows, weavers, oropendolas, and caciques; some American orioles, rockfowl, and others—nest in colonies. So does the Rook, a European crow whose colonial habits gave us the word *rookery*. Nesting in a colony is one way of staying close to your food supply. Wattled Starlings in Africa nest in colonies near locust outbreaks. Group defense provides another motive. On islands in the Amazon, Yellow-rumped Caciques increase the odds against monkeys and other nest raiders by building their colonies near the nests of stinging wasps. For extra insurance, the colonies contain a mixture of active and abandoned nests, thereby subjecting any egg-eating invader to a variant of the old shell game.

What the birds-of-paradise are to plumage, the colonial weavers are to nest building. Many weaver nests are tied together with real knots—simple knots, slip knots, or half hitches, depending on the species. The weavers' ability to weave allows them to attach their nests to the ends of long, thin branches, often over water, where predators cannot reach, and to fix their

entrances (in some species, at least) with long entrance tubes, hanging down two feet (60 cm) or more in the Baya Weaver of Asia and the Black-throated Malimbe of Africa. Even the most agile and light-bodied predator has difficulty negotiating one of these. With these advantages, the weavers have spread widely and successfully. The largest weaver genus, *Ploceus*, has forty-eight species in Africa, five in tropical Asia, and two in Madagascar.

The nests of weavers, like the plumes of the birds-of-paradise, are central to their courtship. Many colonial weavers are polygynous. Weaving is the job of the male, and a Village Weaver can construct his elaborate pouch in a day. He starts by hanging a vertical ring big enough for him to sit in comfortably, then he builds the top of the ring outward to form a roof and works downward to add the walls of the egg chamber, an antechamber, and a short entrance tube. Experience counts—older birds are better builders than their younger rivals.

Like the bower of a bowerbird, a weaver's nest is his chief lure for a mate. An unmated female will not choose a male without a finished nest. The males in a weaver colony do their best to tempt females with their skill, hanging from the entrance of their prospective homes, calling and flapping their wings. In India, Black-breasted and Streaked Weavers add to their allure by daubing wet mud on the nest chamber and planting it with brightly colored flowers and petals. Once a female moves in—signaling her acceptance by bringing soft grasses to line the nest—the male is off to build another for a different mate, while she lays her eggs and raises her brood alone.

Male weavers are not the only birds to court their females with an attractive nest. House

The woven purses built by weaver birds, bound together with real knots, may be the most complex and elegant of bird nests. Many, like this Baya Weaver of southern Asia, add a long entrance tube, making it hard for any but the rightful owners to enter the nest.

Wrens, Great Tits, and other hole-nesting birds claim a site first, then attempt to attract a female to it. A male Yellow-hooded Blackbird will start a nest, then leave it for a female to finish; if she accepts, he starts another, until he has up to five mates. Male Winter, Marsh, and Sedge Wrens build a whole series of incomplete "dummy" nests. Females apparently prefer the male with the largest available number for her consideration. Galápagos finches will even display from the occupied nests of other species of birds.

Many songbirds—House Wrens, tits, nuthatches, Prothonotary Warblers, Australian treecreepers, and others—nest in a hollow limb or a hole in a tree. Few, however, can excavate their own cavities, though the heavy beak of the Finch-billed Myna of Sulawesi may be for digging nest holes, and the White-throated Treerunner, a nuthatchlike ovenbird from the forests of Patagonia, hammers out a cavity nest up to a foot (30 cm) deep. Most cavity-nesting songbirds have to make do with what nature, or at least other birds such as woodpeckers, can provide.

If natural cavities or woodpecker holes are in short supply, Great Tits may take over the available ones, and even kill the smaller Blue Tits in the process. Both Great Tits and Blue Tits will kill Collared Flycatchers for the same reason. House Wrens puncture the eggs of other birds nesting in cavities nearby, perhaps to free up additional nest sites. Marsh Wrens build their own nests, but they, too, regularly break the eggs of other birds in their nesting area, perhaps to drive them away. Probably as a result, Marsh Wren eggs have unusually thick and strong shells.

European Starlings are aggressive pirates of cavity nests, particularly those of bluebirds. Nicholas Collias, an authority on the nests of birds, once saw a starling in Ohio "seize a flicker by the tail and cast it out of the flicker's freshly dug tree cavity, in which a pair of Starlings subsequently nested and reared a brood." European Nuthatches guard against evictions by starlings by plastering mud around the entrance to their nest hole until it is too small for the larger birds to enter.

Cavity nests are not the only ones to suffer from pirates. In Argentina, the ovens of Rufous Horneros are coveted by Brown-chested Martins and introduced House Sparrows, who will go to great lengths to evict the rightful owners. The Chestnut Sparrow normally takes over the nest of another African finch, rather than building one of its own. While most American orioles construct beautiful hanging nests, the Troupial of northern South America—Venezuela's national bird—takes over the nests of Yellow-rumped Caciques or Rufous-fronted Thornbirds instead. In a cacique colony it will evict the birds nesting around it, possibly to give a predator the impression that its corner of the colony is abandoned and not worth searching. Caciques and oropendolas also suffer raids by the Piratic Flycatcher, which harasses the larger birds until they desert. Almost every oropendola colony in Panama contains a pair.

Rufous-fronted Thornbirds build large multichambered stick nests. They nest in one chamber only, but repeatedly enter the others—perhaps to mislead a searching predator. In Venezuela, eleven other species nest or roost in thornbird nests, often while the thornbirds themselves are still in residence in one of the other chambers. Sometimes the birds tolerate one another, but Saffron Finches are often aggressive toward the rightful owners, and Troupials steal eggs, remove sticks from the nest, and otherwise harass the thornbirds enough to be responsible for many nesting failures. Strangely enough, though, thornbirds may do better overall with their other associates than without them, probably because their tenants actually guard the nest more aggressively than do the builders themselves.

The next evolutionary step after stealing another bird's nest is to make the bird raise your young for you. Many songbirds will sneak an egg into the nest of a neighbor. One in ten House Sparrow clutches in Australia, and one in four European Starling nests in New Jersey and the United Kingdom, contain eggs laid by other females.

Laying eggs in the nests of other birds is called *brood parasitism*. Some birds have taken it up as a way of life. The Common Cuckoo of Europe, which is not a songbird, is the classic example. Among songbirds, the only brood parasites that never nest on their own are the whydahs, indigobirds, and the Parasitic Weaver of Africa, and the cowbirds of the New World.

Whydahs and indigobirds are specialists. Each concentrates its efforts on a single host species in its own family. The Northern Paradise-Whydah lays only in the nests of the Green-winged

Pytilia or Melba Finch, the Straw-tailed Whydah in the nest of the Purple Grenadier, and the Village Indigobird in the nest of Jameson's Firefinch.

Cowbirds may have started as specialists. The Bay-winged Cowbird of southern South America usually takes over other birds' nests, but raises its own young. The Screaming Cowbird, though it occasionally lays in the nests of other blackbirds, usually parasitizes only Bay-winged Cowbirds.

The Giant Cowbird parasitizes the nests of its relatives, the oropendolas and caciques. Most of these birds will chase Giant Cowbirds out of their colonies. However, according to one study in Panama, some Chestnut-headed Oropendolas may accept a Giant Cowbird egg without complaint. Young oropendolas may be infested with maggots, but cowbird chicks pluck the maggots off their nest mates and eat them. In colonies built near nests of stinging wasps, maggot-producing flies stay away and oropendolas chase the cowbirds off. However, in trees without wasp nests where the flies can establish a foothold, cowbirds are apparently tolerated. This remarkable situation has not been found among other oropendolas the Giant Cowbird parasitizes, and remains something of a mystery.

The more advanced cowbirds, though, have many potential hosts. The Shiny Cowbird has spread north from South America through the Lesser Antilles to Puerto Rico, and, most recently, South Florida. As it advanced, it laid its eggs in the nests of seventeen West Indian species that had never encountered a brood parasite before. In Puerto Rico, its advent has driven the once-common Yellow-shouldered Blackbird into a few refuges on outlying islands. With no previous experience, the blackbird was totally unable to defend its nest against cowbirds. It still has not learned to recognize its enemy; the two species even roost together.

Brown-headed Cowbirds lay their eggs in the nests of more than a hundred other species. A female can slip into a nest, deposit its egg, and be away in less than a minute. Red-eyed Vireos, Hooded Warblers, and Summer Tanagers may have more than three-quarters of their nests parasitized. On the other hand, Yellow-breasted Chats, Louisiana Waterthrushes, and Eastern Phoebes hardly suffer at all from cowbirds. Either their nests are too hard to find, or if a cowbird does find them the parents will toss out the eggs. Cowbirds in Ontario may try to parasitize

House Finches, but they are making a mistake. The finches feed their young on weed seeds, and on that diet the young cowbirds die in a few days.

Cedar Waxwings, Warbling Vireos, and Baltimore Orioles puncture cowbird eggs or break them in pieces. A Yellow Warbler may desert its nest if a cowbird lays in it. However, it has also developed a more striking defense. If it finds a cowbird egg in its nest, it may simply bury its entire clutch, then build a new nest floor over the top of its eggs and lay a new clutch in the upper story. In South America, the Yellow-browed Tyrant will do the same thing if it is parasitized by Shiny Cowbirds. Shiny Cowbirds, though, can be remarkably persistent. One Rufous Hornero nest held thirty-seven cowbird eggs, laid by a number of different females. Only five were still fresh.

A bird can lay more eggs than she usually does. Take one away, and she will lay another. Brown-headed Cowbirds can lay an egg a day for a month—sometimes up to seventy in a season. But a bird that raises her own young may need to keep some laying potential in reserve in case a predator destroys her first brood. Besides, there may be little point in laying more eggs than she and her mate can feed—though many birds, such as Common Grackles, often do, perhaps because there will occasionally be enough food to raise them all. Otherwise, some of the nestlings die. Nestling Black-billed Magpies are often killed and even eaten by their own nest mates.

Most North American songbirds lay roughly four to five eggs per clutch, though if the season is long enough many will nest again. Birds that nest in holes or especially well-protected places may lay more eggs, possibly because they are less likely to lose them to a predator. White-breasted Nuthatches and Golden-crowned Kinglets may lay eight or nine. Chickadees may lay more. Gray-headed Chickadee clutches may reach fifteen.

Nest predation may be very high in the Tropics. Eighty percent of Bicolored Antbird nests fail in Panama. On the other hand, the breeding season is very long. Many tropical rainforest songbirds lay only two eggs per clutch, but may raise as many as six broods in a season. White-bearded Manakins raise from three to five broods a year. By laying a few eggs at a time but raising several broods a season, a tropical bird increases the chance that at least some of her young will

Yellow Warblers will abandon their nests, or build a new nest floor on top of their old one, to avoid raising a cowbird. Some Yellow Warblers, like this one, still end up rearing young Brown-headed Cowbirds, whose size and demands rapidly outstrip those of the warbler's own chicks.

make it to adulthood. The small tropical tanagers known as euphonias do lay four or five eggs. Pairs of Yellow-throated Euphonias in Costa Rica visit the nest together and arrive only at long intervals, perhaps to avoid revealing their large broods to a watching predator.

A Superb Lyrebird lays only one egg a year, but devotes a remarkable amount of attention to it. The egg takes six weeks to hatch, and it is another six weeks before the chick emerges from the nest. Once it fledges, she continues to feed it, up to 138 times a day—all with no help from the male.

In songbirds, incubation is often the female's job, though most songbird males—211 out of 250 in North America—either feed the female while she is incubating or take their own turn on the nest. When Red Crossbills breed in winter, they cannot leave their eggs uncovered even for a moment. The female sits on them continuously, and if the male did not bring her food, she would starve. On the Arctic tundra, the Snow Bunting's covered nest cools down more quickly than the Lapland Longspur's open cup, whose contents can be warmed by the sun, so the female bunting needs—and gets—the male's help, while the longspur does not. On the other hand, many Australian grassfinches do not incubate at all in the heat of the day.

Newly hatched songbird chicks—unlike those of ducks or chickens—can do little more than beg for food. Songbirds usually hatch with only a few scattered downy feathers, though a few passerines, such as the Black-faced Antthrush, emerge with a full coat of down. Their eyes are sealed shut. During their first week, they must be brooded by their parents because they cannot regulate their own body temperatures. This kind of slow development, which is called *altricial*, may be necessary because so much of songbird behavior has to be learned, and learning takes time. We see the same sort of thing in our own species.

Once the young hatch, the parent birds work overtime to feed them. The Great Tit has been recorded making 990 trips per day to its nest, while in North America House Wrens may make almost five hundred trips per day. Pied Flycatchers visit their nest box with food every two minutes, making for a total of 6,200 trips between hatching and fledging.

The Lapland Longspur nests on the Arctic tundra in both the New and the Old Worlds. Because females can leave the nest to be warmed by the sun, male longspurs—unlike male Snow Buntings—do not help with incubation.

The young birds, in their turn, stimulate their parents' efforts with begging cries. European Starling parents favor the nestling that, as Elizabeth Litovich and Harry Power write, "chirps the loudest, gapes the widest, stretches its neck the longest and flaps its wings the most." Fleshy wattles decorate the corners of many nestling beaks, colorful targets to show the parents where to deliver their food. A begging Gouldian Finch chick reveals a mouth highlighted in the corners by three opalescent green-and-blue spots. Each species of African weaver finch has its own distinctively patterned mouth lining. The chicks of indigobirds ensure being fed by mimicking the distinctive mouth linings of their hosts.

The food that adult birds eat is not necessarily what they feed their nestlings. Nestlings need protein to grow and develop, and may not be able to get it from adult foods, especially fruit. Many, but not all, fruit-eating birds feed insects to their young. Lapland Longspurs give their chicks the calcium they need by supplementing their diet of craneflies and sawflies with lemming bones and teeth.

Nestlings excrete the results of their meals in gelatinous capsules called *fecal sacs*. Many songbirds carefully remove their chicks' fecal sacs, or even eat them (particularly when the chicks are young and their digestive powers incomplete) to recycle the nutrients. Fecal sacs may provide nesting White-crowned Sparrows with 10 percent of their daily energy requirements. On the other hand, finches like the Goldfinch, Bullfinch, or House Finch—members of the cardueline group—make no such effort, and by the end of the nesting period their nests are quite foul. For some Australian grass finches, beetles living in the nests act as a sort of cleanup crew. Cactus Wrens may leave the white residue to reflect away the desert heat.

Many birds go to great trouble to avoid being seen as they head back to the nest with their catch. Meadowlarks land some distance away, then sneak quietly home through the grass. In European marshes, the Bearded Reedling pretends to look for food as it works its way closer to where its nest hangs suspended from marsh stems. Though Hudson's Canastero carefully conceals its nest in pampas bushes, its efforts may be undone by its young. W. H. Hudson, for whom the canastero was named, found that the Chimango Caracara, a sort of falcon, fed its young exclusively on canastero nestlings it found by listening for their "stridulous laughter." Hudson marveled at this species,

> *in the fashioning and perfecting of which Nature seems to have exhausted all her art, so exquisitely is it adapted in its structure, coloration, and habits to the one great object of concealment, yet apparently doomed to destruction through this one petty oversight—the irrepressible garrulity of the fledglings in their nest!*

Young birds hatch already knowing some surprising things. The Greater Kiskadee, a species of tyrant flycatcher that ranges from Texas to southern South America, can recognize some poisonous snakes from the moment it hatches. That aside, what a young bird experiences very early

A Gouldian Finch chick has three bright opalescent spots at the corner of its mouth. They may act like landing lights on an airfield, guiding the parents to the right place to deliver food.

in life may determine how it behaves ever afterward. Imprinting, only possible in early infancy, determines where a Zebra Finch builds its nest and what materials it uses to make it, or how a Loggerhead Shrike impales its prey on a thorn.

The period of relatively helpless infancy is usually short. Young Indigo Buntings leave the nest after only nine to twelve days. The first weeks after a songbird leaves its nest are usually the most dangerous of its life. Its chance of making it through to the end of its first year is generally only about half that of an adult. Predators may destroy half of all songbird nests, but, once fledged, starvation is a young bird's greatest enemy. Only 11 percent of Yellow-eyed Juncos banded as nestlings reappear after migration the following spring. Only 40 percent of Florida Scrub Jays, which do not migrate, survive their first year.

Risks or no, young songbirds, like young mammals, may spend a good deal of time playing. Crows play "king of the mountain" or "follow the leader." Young Great Tits play "tag" on the wing, and Jungle Babblers rough-and-tumble on the ground. House Sparrows drop stones from rooftops, apparently to hear them fall. When a young Garden Warbler discovered that it could make a ringing sound by dropping a pebble in a glass someone had left nearby, other youngsters took up the game and made it into a group activity.

By the time it fledges, a nestling's natal down has been replaced by a full set of feathers, their immature plumage. At its next molt, it usually emerges in adult garb—but male Red-winged Blackbirds, Baltimore Orioles, Scarlet Tanagers, American Redstarts, and nearly thirty other North American songbirds take at least a year to gain full adult plumage. Birds-of-paradise may take several years. One-year-old male redstarts look like females, but can establish territories, mate, and raise young. By delaying their full male plumage, they may avoid attacks from older males.

Fledgling Indigo Buntings, like most temperate songbirds, stay with their parents for three weeks after leaving the nest. In the Tropics, the family may stay together for much longer—sometimes for as long as twenty-three weeks. Once young Spotted Antbirds leave the nest, the adults divide parental duties, each parent taking charge of one of their two fledglings. Even if one chick dies, the parent guarding it rarely feeds its remaining offspring.

For roughly 220 species of birds, the young may not leave home at all. Instead, they stay to help their parents raise a new brood, or join in defending a communal territory with a number of relatives. A pair of Florida Scrub Jays may have up to six helpers defending their territory, protecting and feeding the nestlings, and fighting off a nestling jay's worst enemy, snakes. A group of Southern Pied Babblers in Namibia worked together to kill one of their predators, a Gabar Goshawk.

Why do helpers help, rather than setting up on their own? Young birds may not be able to establish a territory until an older pair dies or disappears. Scrub Jay helpers are at least defending and feeding their younger brothers and sisters, who do share some of their genes. In Mexican Jays, though, more than one pair in the territory may nest, and the helpers may not be the breeding pair's offspring. A young Henderson Island Reed Warbler in the South Pacific may help a completely unrelated pair, perhaps because trios have better luck getting territories.

More than sixty species of communal nesters live in Australia. Three of the six Australian treecreepers are usually found in trios, two breeding birds and a helper. The Superb Fairy-Wren, or Blue Wren, employs up to four helpers, usually young males from earlier broods. Young males apparently stay to help because Blue Wren males outnumber females and there are not enough mates to go around. The helpers join in guarding their territory, even singing with the breeding birds. They preen one another, and help feed the young both in and out of the nest. With helpers on hand, a breeding pair can nest more often than a pair on its own. Without helpers, Blue Wrens usually raise one or two young a year. With them, that number rises from two to eight.

Communal nesting is commonest in dry, warm country—much of Australia, for example—where food may be hard to find, birds are resident year-round, and space and resources are at a premium. Helpers may leave and set up on their own if they can. When they cannot, they are better off staying put, joining—as Australians call one communally nesting species, the Gray-crowned Babbler—a "Happy Family."

HOME GARDENS, FOREIGN FIELDS

There are two ways to see birds. You can go to them, or you can entice them to come to you.

A properly planned and planted garden can be a nature refuge all its own. With a bit of planning, you can provide a refuge and a resource for many kinds of birds—and a wonderful educational experience for your children. Considering what many of our cities and suburbs are like, it may well be an oasis.

A bird garden should have two purposes (besides beauty and pleasure): to provide shelter and food. That means selecting some plants (such as spruce or cotoneaster) that provide the dense cover many birds need, and others (such as mountain ash or sumac) that produce nutritious crops of fruit. Variety should be your watchword—and, of course, keep your garden pesticide-free (birds eat insect pests, too).

Your garden may entice birds to nest there. You can increase the odds of that happening by putting up nest boxes. Remember, though, that a closed-in nest box will be of interest only to birds that normally breed in cavities or covered nests. House Wrens, chickadees, and bluebirds are prime tenants. Other birds, such as American Robins or Barn Swallows, will nest in a birdhouse only if one or more of its sides are left open—they may prefer the eaves of your house to a home of their own.

You are unlikely, of course, to have a bird-of-paradise in your back garden. Today, though, exotic birds are increasingly within reach of travelers with a taste for adventure and a reasonably deep pocket. One of the greatest advantages to being a naturalist, after all, is that there is no such thing as an uninteresting place to visit.

A number of companies will now take you to the farthest reaches of the globe, in the company of often astonishingly knowledgeable experts, with the single-minded aim of showing you every species of bird that it is humanly possible to find. You can find their ads in almost any nature or birding magazine. If such hard-core group birding treks are not for you, there are guest lodges in some delightful places that cater especially to birders, or at least to naturalists. The Asa Wright Nature Centre in Trinidad, O'Reilly's Guest House at the edge of Lamington National Park in southern Queensland, and the Mile High Lodge in the Huachuca Mountains of Arizona are old and established—but far from unique. A few days at O'Reilly's will leave you awash in everything from bowerbirds to bandicoots.

Birding vacations are, or at least should be, part of the increasingly popular kind of travel called *ecotourism*. Proper ecotourism is not just rewarding for you, but good for the wildlife you see. It gives people who live near that wildlife and control its destiny a reason to value and protect their animals and plants.

Unfortunately, not everything that calls itself ecotourism deserves the name. If this is your kind of travel, you should be careful to choose green travel that is really green. The Ecotourism Society has defined *real* ecotourism as "purposeful travel to natural areas to understand the culture and natural history of the environment, taking care not to alter the integrity of the ecosystem, while producing economic opportunities that make the conservation of natural resources beneficial to local people." That doesn't apply, for instance, to building a luxury hotel at the edge of a rainforest, funneling so many people down a nature trail that the wildlife along it is disrupted, or pushing local people aside to protect the profits of distant tour operators.

There are better alternatives, and with a little investigation you should be able to find places where—just as in the nature reserve you can create in your own yard—your enjoyment of wildlife can benefit the birds you see, while it enriches your own life.

THE APPETITE OF A BIRD

"Is it weakness of intellect, birdie?" I cried,
"Or a rather tough worm in your little inside?"

—W. S. GILBERT, *THE MIKADO*

A Black-capped Chickadee puts its agility to good use, whether hanging acrobatically from a twig as it probes for food, or, as here, hovering in flight to drink from a dripping icicle.

The Black-capped Chickadee's diet changes with the seasons. In summer, 90 percent of its food is animal matter, mostly caterpillars and spiders. In the fall, it dines on waxy fruits of poison ivy and bayberry. In winter, half its daily intake is coniferous seeds and other plant material. In the earliest spring it hovers in the air, picking icicles of sap that drip from maple branches. Less picturesquely, it pecks for fat at the carcasses of deer and other animals, even at dead fish. The Black-capped Chickadee is, in short, a resourceful and flexible generalist. Chickadees glean their prey from leaves and twigs, hanging upside down to get at hard-to-reach items; probe for them in cracks and crevices; hawk them from a leaf or twig with a short flight; or sally out to snap them from midair. Chickadees even learn the best places to find food by observing others. Watch a chickadee, and you will see much of the behavior any small songbird might use in search of its food.

Many small, insect-eating songbirds glean, or probe, or hawk, or sally, but few do them all. A Least Flycatcher sallies for flying insects, while a Black-and-white Warbler explores the bark of trunks and large limbs. Tropical songbirds may be even more specialized, such as the

On Wenman Island in the Galápagos, the Sharp-
beaked Ground-Finch has developed the habit of
pecking at the feather bases of seabirds like these
Masked Boobies to draw blood, a behavior that
has earned them the nickname "vampire finch."

Buffy Tuftedcheeks and the Jamaican Blackbirds that hunt creatures living in the bromeliads that cling to the limbs of rainforest trees.

Other songbirds shift their diet from season to season, too. An Eastern Kingbird eats a surprising amount of fruit on its wintering grounds. Though Rufous-collared Sparrows in Chile eat seeds for most of the year, in the cool, wet July winter they switch about half their diet to insects, and their digestive tract actually grows in length and weight to handle the change.

What a bird eats is determined by, and in the long evolutionary term determines, its body shape, bill type, and behavior. Its choice may depend literally on how much it can cram into its mouth. In Australia, Noisy Friarbirds eat cicadas that their cousins the Red Wattlebirds ignore, probably because they can gape more widely and are better able to stuff such large insects down their gullets. The grotesque hooked beak of the Dusky Broadbill, almost as broad as it is long and wider than the bird's skull, may help it manage prey like lizards and large grasshoppers. The broad bill and huge gape of American bellbirds may help them swallow large fruits.

The bigger its beak, the wider the size range of foods a bird can eat. Birds on islands, where the absence of competitors allows them to take a broader selection of foods, may have longer or heavier beaks than their mainland relatives. Tahiti Reed Warblers, Blue Mountain Vireos on Jamaica, and the massively billed (and extinct) Bonin Grosbeak are all results of this evolutionary shift.

Island birds may feed in most unsongbirdlike ways. On Laysan atoll in the far northwestern Hawaiian Islands, the Laysan Finch scavenges abandoned eggs and the dead bodies of albatrosses and Sooty Terns. On Wenman Island in the Galápagos, Sharp-beaked Ground-Finches do not wait for the birds to die. They peck open the growing pinfeathers of seabird nestlings and drink their blood.

Galápagos finches are particularly resourceful at inventing new ways to get at food. The Small Ground-Finch and the Large Cactus-Finch can move stones more than ten times their own weight by placing their heads against a rock and using their whole body as a living crowbar, prying the stones from their beds with their feet.

On remote Inaccessible Island in the South Atlantic, Tristan Thrushes catch kelp flies on the boulder-strewn shoreline. So do Savannah Sparrows on the San Benitos Islands of Baja California. The Seaside Cinclodes, a mainland ovenbird of the Pacific coast of South America, dashes back and forth in the surf like a small sandpiper, snatching up tiny marine animals exposed by the waves. On the Falklands, its cousin the Blackish Cinclodes, or Tussock Bird, will eat almost anything it can get, including cracked penguin eggs, beach fleas, carrion, and the leavings of the islanders, which it will enter their houses to steal.

The challenge most insect-eating birds face—and the spur to many of their anatomical adaptations—is not how to handle the insects once they have caught them, but how to get at them in the first place. They must reach into their hiding places, scratch them from the soil and the leaf litter, snatch them in flight, or flush them into the open. They need keen eyesight, perhaps strong legs and feet for scratching, just the right sort of bill, and finely tuned responses. Even the relatively simple task of picking a caterpillar from a leaf requires balance, agility, and the ability to focus on just the right spot—which means that the bill must be long enough to bring its tip into the bird's field of binocular vision.

We have space to look at only some of the more extreme of these adaptations. The Recurve-billed Bushbird, an antbird from Amazonia, has a peculiar blade-shaped bill with a strongly upturned lower mandible. It uses it to split open the stems of heliconias, rainforest plants related to bananas and bird-of-paradise flowers.

The special features of some songbird bills are adapted not so much to close the mandibles but to open them. European Starlings and many American blackbirds gape to spread apart mats of grass or open curled-up leaves as they hunt. Starlings in my backyard do the same thing to pry open a shutter designed to keep squirrels away from my bird feeder. The ultimate gaper is the Scarlet-headed Blackbird of the temperate marshes of South America. The Federal, as the Argentines call it, has a bill like the blade of a chisel. It uses it to split open thick-stemmed bulrushes, then gapes to force the stems open, using muscles attached to a huge process on the back of its lower jaw.

No songbird can drill into a tree with the skill and thoroughness of a woodpecker, though nuthatches and creepers are every bit as accomplished, if not more so, at maneuvering on a vertical trunk. Woodpeckers, however, are not found everywhere, and where they are absent songbirds have come up with some interesting substitutes. The Huia and the Akiapolaau we have already met. On woodpecker-free Madagascar, the Sickle-billed Vanga uses its long, curved beak to extract insect larvae from holes or crevices in trees.

On remote Inaccessible Island in the South Atlantic, the Tristan Thrush forages along the seashore, even pausing to inspect the occasional dead fish.

Woodpeckers are completely absent from Australasia, where their place is partly taken—at least in the rainforests of New Guinea and Australia—by long-billed birds-of-paradise such as the Brown Sicklebill and the Queen Victoria's Riflebird. Australian gum trees shed their bark in long strips, and the Crested Shriketit tears at them with its thick, powerful bill, exposing the insects beneath.

A number of songbirds deliberately flush their prey. In tropical Asia and Australasia, fantails spread their long tails, flashing white outer tail feathers, as they hunt for insects. Their twitching tails may help startle insects into revealing themselves. In North America, the American Redstart does much the same thing, displaying patches of orange or yellow as it flicks its tail open and shut. The Pied Monarch of the northern Australian rainforests is a striking black-and-white bird with an erectile white neck ruff. It hunts in a most extraordinary way, landing on a tree trunk with wings and tail spread and frill erect, beating about until it startles an insect into movement, then snatching its prey or sallying out to catch it in flight.

For whole-body adaptation, consider the dippers. The two South American species wade only belly-deep in the water, but their Northern Hemisphere cousins the American, White-throated, and Brown Dippers plunge directly into rushing mountain streams, using their wings to swim to the bottom. Here, on dives up to thirty seconds long, they explore for the larvae of caddisflies, blackflies, and mayflies, for freshwater shrimp and fish, and for other small water creatures.

Most carnivorous songbirds are too small to eat much besides insects, spiders, and such. Black Phoebes will, though, occasionally plunge into shallow water to catch small fish. Giant Pittas eat frogs and small snakes. Jays are notorious nest robbers, and the largest of the ovenbirds, the Brown Cacholote, will even raid poultry yards, driving the hens from their nests with loud cries and stealing their eggs. An enterprising Common Grackle killed and ate thirty-five White-throated Sparrows, a Ruby-crowned Kinglet, an Ovenbird, and a House Sparrow during a few spring weeks in a parkette in downtown Toronto.

Size is not a problem for crows and ravens. Ravens are traditional pickers of bones, even of our own species. In Florida, Common Crows band together to rob meals from Great Egrets, White Ibis, Turkey Vultures, otters, or even squirrels. American Crows themselves are robbed by Northern Ravens in New Hampshire. Australian crows and ravens attack dying lambs, and on both continents crows and ravens invade colonies of cormorants to plunder their nests. Their depredations may be a major contributor to declines in cormorant populations.

The hooked, notched bill of a shrike recalls a small falcon, though the shrike lacks the talons of a true bird of prey. Northern Hemisphere shrikes, and two species in Africa, store the mice and small birds they catch by impaling them on thorns or twists of barbed wire. Shrikes are often called "butcherbirds," but that name really belongs to an unrelated group of Australian birds with even larger and more impressive bills. Australian butcherbirds also impale their catches, or wedge them into the fork of a branch.

Though many songbirds are vegetarians, hardly any eat leaves. Leaves are high in bulk, low

A Northern Shrike uses a "larder" to store its prey, either wedging its kills into crevices between branches or impaling them on thorns.

Plantcutters are South American members of the cotinga family with specially serrated bills they use to snip away buds and shoots. The White-tipped Plantcutter is considered a pest by orchard growers in Chile.

in nutrition, and full of cellulose. Horses and cows have parts of their digestive systems set aside as macerating chambers for the leaves they eat. So does the Hoatzin, a strange nonsongbird from South America. A small bird, however, cannot afford to carry so much dead weight. One of the few songbirds that does eat leaves, the Kokako of New Zealand, is a heavy-bodied, weak-flying relative of the unfortunate Huia. Even Kokakos confine their attentions to tender young leaves, and vary their diet with fruit and the occasional invertebrate.

Buds are another matter. Rose-breasted Grosbeaks are confirmed bud eaters. So are the plantcutters, peculiar suboscines that make themselves the bane of orchard growers in Chile by snipping away buds, tender shoots, and fruit, with bills serrated like the blade of a tiny saw.

Yellow-rumped Warblers and Tree Swallows that winter far north along the Atlantic coast survive, like chickadees in fall, by eating large numbers of bayberries. The birds can digest their waxy coatings, an adaptation that allows them to bypass the dangers of the long flight south forced upon their relatives, which lack it.

Fruit is nutritious, attractive, and digestible—and for good reason. Plants with edible fruit use it as bait, drawing in animals that may disperse their seeds. In New Guinea, there are fruits that only birds-of-paradise and a few fruit-doves seem able to eat. Encased in hard shells other birds cannot pry open, they are four to five times more nutritious than less recalcitrant fruits. Birds-of-paradise tend to scatter seeds evenly through the forest, instead of excreting them all in one place, and so may be better servants of the plants than less exotic fruit eaters.

Fruit can be hard to reach, and it pays for a fruit-eating tanager to be an acrobat.

Many songbirds will eat fruit when they can get it, even if insects form the main part of their diet. Here, an Omao, or Hawaiian Thrush, plucks a pilo berry.

Ornithologist Steven Hilty has noticed that tropical tanagers are much better at picking fruit than Swainson's Thrush, a migrant from the North that eats a lot of fruit in winter but is far less elegant in getting at it.

Phainopeplas, Australian Mistletoebirds, euphonias, and some tyrant flycatchers specialize on mistletoe berries. A euphonia can—indeed, must—pass a mistletoe berry completely through its gut in seven or eight minutes. The seed inside is coated with sticky, toxic slime. A quick passage through its digestive system ensures that the euphonia digests only the nutritious outer layer. The bird excretes the seeds, and their coating, in long, glutinous strands, often wiping itself on a branch to get rid of them—thereby, inadvertently, depositing the mistletoe seeds in the best spot for these parasitic plants, high in a tree.

Fruits that attract birds may help the plant. Seeds are another matter. A bird that eats them destroys the plant's chance to reproduce. Many seeds have hard, thick coats that challenge any bird. Songbirds, of course, have met the challenge. Jays and chickadees hammer seeds open, holding them down with their feet as they work. Nuthatches wedge nuts into a crevice before hack-

A male Mistletoebird delivers a mistletoe berry to its young. Mistletoebirds can be found anywhere in Australia where mistletoes grow, from rainforest to desert.

ing (or "hatching") them open. Grosbeaks rely on heavy, thick beaks and strong jaw muscles. Ridges and grooves on the inside of a finch's bill hold the seed in place while the bird moves its lower jaw back and forth to saw it open, or crushes it by main force. An Evening Grosbeak, or its Eurasian equivalent, the Hawfinch, can crack a cherry pit.

The trick is to get rid of the seed coat without dropping the nutritious bits. A Northern Cardinal can shell a hemp seed, which has a particularly hard outer coat, in 13.5 seconds. Smaller birds are better at handling seeds such as millet. Red-browed, Beautiful, and Diamond Firetails in Western Australia prefer small, narrow grass seeds that are relatively easy to husk. An American Tree Sparrow can husk a millet seed in less than half the time it takes the larger White-throated Sparrow.

Large, medium-sized, and small seed eaters, then, can focus their attention on a particular range of seed size and hardness. The Black-bellied Seedcracker, a rich crimson-and-black bird of African tropical forests, has a bill that comes in three sizes. Birds with all three bill types live together, each specializing in a different range of seeds.

Pinyon Jays and Clark's Nutcrackers, large birds with strong, pointed bills, chisel their way into the cones of pinyon pines to extract their seeds. Crossbills are more surgical in their approach, slipping the crossed tips of their bills into a cone, prying the scales apart, and lifting out the seeds with their tongues. Each crossbill specializes in a different conifer type. The largest, the Parrot Crossbill of Eurasia and the Scottish Crossbill of the highlands of Scotland, are pine feeders. In Europe, Red Crossbills prefer spruce, and White-winged Crossbills larch, but in North America, where the larger species are absent and the spruce trees have smaller cones, the Red visits pines and the White-winged moves up to spruce. The only other birds with crossed mandible tips, the Akepa and the Akekee of the

Hawaiian Islands, use their slightly twisted beaks to pry for insects hidden in the buds of forest trees.

Nectar, like some fruit, is supposed to be eaten. Plants produce it to lure their pollinators: birds, bats, butterflies, beetles, flies, or, in some parts of South Africa, even mice. In the New World, avian nectar feeding is dominated by hummingbirds, whose more than three hundred species far outnumber the short list of songbird nectar specialists: honeycreepers, dacnises, flower-piercers, the Orangequit—a nectar-feeding finch confined to Jamaica—and the widespread Bananaquit.

In the Old World, where there are no hummingbirds, the sunbirds rival them in beauty, iridescence, and diet. They visit flowers from Africa to Indonesia. Their only rivals are the South African sugarbirds, which specialize on the spectacular *Protea* flowers and may be giant sunbirds anyway, and the suboscine sunbird-asities of Madagascar. Though only one sunbird reaches Australia, nectar-feeding birds may be more important there than anywhere else. Nectar literally drips from the flowers of eucalypts, melaleucas, banksias, and grevilleas.

An American Goldfinch brandishes its food, the seed of an oyster plant.

The sickle-shaped bill of the Iiwi matches the curved flowers of Hawaiian native lobelias. Since many of the lobelias have become rare, Iiwis have switched to other types of flowers, and their bills appear to have grown shorter over the past century.

One of the largest Australian bird families, the honeyeaters, is highly dependent on it, and many other birds will drink it when they can. I have even watched Australian treecreepers take nectar.

Since a plant gets no benefit from a pollinator unless the pollinator visits another flower of the same species, the plant may keep its nectar out of reach of all but specialists. Among songbirds, that means birds—such as the sunbirds—with long, curved bills and brush-tipped tongues rolled into tubes that look, and function, like soda straws. They, in turn, acquire a food few others can share. The match between a flower's shape and a pollinator's bill can be precise. In Madagascar, the bill of the Common Sunbird-Asity matches a species of Malagasy balsam, *Impatiens humblotiana*. In Hawaii, the bills of the Iiwi and the Mamo fit the flowers of several species of lobelia—or at least they once did. Today, the Mamo is extinct, many of the Hawaiian lobelias are extinct or endangered, and the Iiwi, though still locally common, tends to have a shorter bill than it did a century ago. Instead of lobelias, Iiwis today are more likely to visit the brushlike flowers of the ohia lehua.

In East Africa, the flowers of the mint *Leonotis* match the long, curved bill of the Golden-winged Sunbird. Golden-winged Sunbirds can extract as much as 90 percent of a *Leonotis*'s nectar. The Malachite Sunbird has

A Masked Flower-piercer tears into the base of a flower to steal nectar, robbing the plant by bypassing its pollen—the reason that the flower developed nectar in the first place.

a straighter bill, and must jab its way into the flower, collecting only 82 percent of the nectar. The Variable Sunbird, a smaller species with a short bill, bypasses the whole process— and the flower's pollen—by stabbing through the floral base from the outside. The Variable can make off with only 62 percent of the nectar available—and it cheats the plant by bypassing its pollen.

The tropical American flower-piercers are professional cheats. They have a thin bill that ends in a sharp hook, perfect for tearing its way through the base of a flower to get at the nectar inside.

What about water? In the deserts of central Australia thousands of honeyeaters, finches, and other birds visit water holes every day. Swallows, which need water for sustained flight, dip low over a pond to snatch a beakful as they fly past. Black-capped Chickadees may eat snow in winter. Most songbirds, though, do not have to drink. Birds that eat insects can usually get enough water from the bodies of their prey. Seed eaters have more of a problem, but the Australian

The Black-spotted Bare-Eye of the western Amazon is an antbird that truly deserves its name; it is rarely found away from swarms of army ants. Like other ant followers, it does not eat the ants themselves, but snaps up other insects flushed by the advancing column.

Zebra Finch and the African Scaly-feathered Finch can live on seeds, even with less than 10 percent water content, by recycling the water they get as a byproduct of their digestion.

The quest for food has driven songbirds into some strange associations. Long columns of army ants march through the rainforests of tropical America, devouring anything too small or weak to get out of their path. In Africa, blind driver ants feel their way through the forest in such numbers that they wear a furrow as they pass. Ants contain too much formic acid to be a palatable meal for most birds, although some species, such as Australian treecreepers, may specialize in them. On both continents, though, birds specialize in following the ant columns, not to eat the ants themselves but to catch the insects, spiders, and other small creatures scurrying to escape the van of the attacking force.

In Africa, driver ants may be attended by bristlebills, alethes, and antthrushes. In the Americas, twenty-eight species of antbird are full-time ant followers, rarely found away from an army ant column. They have strong legs and feet, ideal for clinging to vertical stems above the ant stream. Woodcreepers, manakins, tanagers, and other birds may join them—even Swainson's Thrush, a bird that could hardly take up this habit on its northern breeding grounds. Where Spotted, Bicolored, and Ocellated Antbirds live together in Central America, the large Ocellated dominates the area closest to the ants, where the pickings are best. The medium-sized Bicolored takes up an intermediate position, while the small Spotted is relegated to the sidelines.

In the forests of southeastern Australia, a number of small birds regularly follow the Superb Lyrebird as it scratches in the soil and snap up small invertebrates disturbed by the larger bird's efforts. One bird does this so regularly that it is called the Pilotbird, a name recalling the pilot fish that accompany sharks. In southeastern South America, groups of the rare Saffron-cowled Blackbird follow a large flycatcher, the Black-and-white Monjita, but no one is too sure why.

Cowbirds get their name from following cattle, watching for insects that they flush from the grass. South American Cattle Tyrants ride capybaras, and the Piapiac, a long-tailed crow, rides

African animals from antelopes to elephants. Red-winged Starlings, Pale-winged Starlings, and Yellow-bellied Bulbuls land on klipspringers, a small African antelope, to hunt for ticks. Red-billed and Yellow-billed Oxpeckers are African starlings that have become so specialized for climbing about on large animals, winnowing their fur for ticks, that they can do little else. They are a familiar accompaniment to a wide range of Africa's ungulates, though elephants, apparently, will not tolerate them.

Chickadees, nuthatches, and other birds travel in mixed-species flocks, searching for food, through the Northern Hemisphere winter. In tropical rainforests, much larger and more organized flocks may stay together year-round.

I have often walked silent rainforest trails, seeing nothing until a rush of birds filled the foliage with brief activity before twittering away into the distance. They might be white-eyes, whistlers, monarchs, and honeyeaters in New Guinea; babblers, bulbuls, fantails, and leafbirds in Borneo; or foliage-gleaners, treehunters, tanagers, and warblers in southeastern Brazil. Newtonias, white-eyes, vangas, Madagascar Paradise-Flycatchers, and the newly discovered Cryptic Warbler join mixed-species flocks in the rainforest of eastern Madagascar, while in the western Amazon flocks of up to seventy species and one hundred individuals—woodcreepers, ovenbirds, flycatchers, tanagers, and others—range the forests together. Even pygmy squirrels will travel with flocks of birds in the New World Tropics. Some birds join a flock as it enters their territory, and leave as it passes out the other side. In Amazonian flocks, others take up permanent membership, and no new member of their species may join as long as their posts are filled.

Not all flocks are identical, even in the same forest. Birds of the high canopy join different flocks from birds such as ant-tanagers and antshrikes, which forage lower down. I have seen canopy flocks and understory flocks pass each other in opposite directions in Costa Rica, like commuters on different lanes of a highway.

Sometimes, birds of a feather really do flock together. In New Guinea, brown and black birds from several different families—Black Cuckooshrikes, pitohuis, manucodes, drongos, and

Many African animals, like this buffalo, will tolerate the attentions of Red-billed Oxpeckers, even when the birds explore seemingly sensitive areas.

more—may form bicolored foraging parties. Flocks of black-and-yellow birds assemble in western Panama. Perhaps their similarities keep the flock together.

Mixed-species flocks often form around from one to six *nuclear species*. In the highlands of Costa Rica, the Sooty-capped Bush-Tanager is a nuclear species for Collared Redstarts, Ruddy Treerunners, and other birds. On Hispaniola, Black-crowned Palm Tanagers may attract resident birds and northern migrants, including Bananaquits, Black-throated Blue Warblers, Stripe-headed Tanagers, and Greater Antillean Pewees. Nuclear species may actually try to gather a flock. In Amazonian Peru, Bluish-slate and Dusky-throated Antshrikes use special calls to rally as many as thirty other species before starting out to forage each morning. As the assembled flock moves through the forest, one of the antshrikes may fly on ahead, calling to the others to catch up.

The activity of all these different sorts of birds probably helps to flush prey, making each bird's hunting easier. In the cloud forests of the mountains of Ecuador, birds are more likely to join flocks in bad weather, when flying insects are probably harder to find. When Fork-tailed Drongos join a mixed flock in Africa, they snap up the insects that other birds have flushed rather than looking for their own. It is harder, too, for a hunter to snatch a bird out of a flock without being noticed than to surprise one on its own—though the Slaty-backed Forest-Falcon, a songbird specialist from tropical America, is said to actually attract flocks of birds by imitating their mobbing calls. The falcon snatches them as they seek it through the dense foliage.

A Eurasian Jay stores between 5,700 and 11,000 acorns each autumn, each in a separate place as insurance in case another bird, or a squirrel, finds them. They form its main food supply over the next ten months. Gray Jays coat each item with a special, sticky saliva secretion, planting their glutinous hoard on a branch, where it dries hard and remains protected until the jay returns. Clark's Nutcracker holds up to ninety pinyon pine seeds in a pouch under its tongue, and may bury thirty-three thousand of them in the soil per year, in caches of four or five seeds each. It reaps the rewards of its work—as does the Pinyon Jay, another seed hoarder—by having enough stored food available to begin breeding in late February, well in advance of most other birds. The Pinyon Jay's seed-eating habits actually benefit the pine; some of its caches go unfound, sprout, and contribute to the tree's spread. That may be why pinyon seeds are unusually large, nutritious, and desirable.

All the Temperate Zone members of the chickadee family, except the Great and the Blue Tits, store seeds. Black-capped Chickadees store their caches in cracks and crevices, curled leaves, knotholes, the hollow ends of broken twigs, or even under roof shingles or in drainpipes. The Crested Tit gets up to 60 percent of its winter food from seed caches. Storage is not necessarily for the long term. Most Marsh Tit caches hide food the birds were simply unable to eat at the time, and they usually return to pick it up within a few hours.

The kind of spatial memory all this requires is mind-boggling. Tits may store between fifty and eighty thousand spruce seeds in a season, each in a different place, and remember where they put each one up to twenty-eight days later. A Clark's Nutcracker can remember where it put about two thousand seed catches for up to eight to nine months.

Chickadees, nuthatches, and crows that store food have a special center in the

The most famous case of avian tool use: A Woodpecker Finch from the Galápagos digs out wood-boring grubs with a cactus spine.

hippocampus of their brains that is devoted to spatial information. Apparently, the bird must actually store the food item itself in order to remember where it is. Chickadees do not seem able to remember where other chickadees have hidden food, even if they have watched them do it. They must eat the fruits of their own labors, not those of their neighbors.

The most remarkable application of the avian brain, though, may be tool use. Some thrushes and pittas break snail shells on a stone "anvil." The Noisy Pitta smashes them on a stone or piece of wood that may become worn from repeated use. The Woodpecker Finch of the Galápagos explores for insects in holes and crevices of branches with a cactus spine or a twig. In Australia, Varied Sittellas use bits of bark to probe for insects. A Great Tit was once seen extracting insect larvae from their retreats with a conifer needle. Captive Marsh Tits peeled strips of colored tape from feeders in their cages, folded them with their bills and feet, and used them to scoop up and store bits of powdered food—and we have already met the New Caledonian Crow, a bird that goes the Woodpecker Finch one better by manufacturing its own tools.

The most abundant songbird in the world: Flocks of Red-billed Queleas come to water in the Okavango delta of Botswana.

To end, two remarkable stories. The Bell Miner of eastern Australia is the most colonial of honeyeaters. Groups of more than thirty birds call repeatedly in their eucalypt forest home, their loud *tink* notes joining in a minimalist chorale that can be pleasantly evocative or maddening, depending on how long you have to listen to it. Bell Miners do not depend on flowers for their sugar fix, but on insects. The nymphs of psyllid bugs tap into the sap of eucalypt trees, secreting the excess sugar as a sort of candy shell called a *lerp*. Bell Miners pretty much live on lerps, but either eat them without swallowing the bug or concentrate on larger psyllids, leaving the young ones to grow. Other birds are not so picky. When experimenters removed an entire colony of Bell Miners, a host of rosellas, pardalotes, thornbills, and other birds invaded its former territory and ate every last bug, lerp and all, within a few weeks. This hadn't happened before because the miners worked together to chase other birds out of their territory. By keeping them away, the miners ensure themselves a ready supply of their favorite food. A Bell Miner territory, in short, is a lerp ranch.

The Red-billed Quelea of Africa is the most abundant land bird on earth. There are at least 750 million of them. It is surely the most gregarious—a quelea colony usually holds about sixty thousand birds. Africans regard this little weaver as a plague second only to the migratory locust, a menace to be fought with every weapon available, including flamethrowers. Although they may descend in the hundreds of thousands on fields of sorghum, millet, rice, wheat, or barley, queleas may not be the horrendous pest they have been portrayed to be. For some Africans they are a welcome source of food, and their guano is used as fertilizer in Nigeria. Though they certainly cause devastating local damage to crops, in total they probably destroy less than 1 percent of Africa's cereal production.

Red-billed Queleas depend almost entirely on grass seeds, and that need forces them into a life of wandering. In the dry season they can find seeds in plenty. Once the rains come, however, the remaining seeds sprout, the grass begins a new cycle of growth and flowering, and the queleas must move or die. In southern Africa, perhaps half of them starve to death each winter. The survivors must find an area that is still dry, or one where the rainy season is coming to an end and masses of fresh seeds and insect larvae are available for the eating. Here, after a journey of at least 185 miles (300 km), they breed—as quickly as possible, incubating their eggs for only about eleven days and fledging their young after another thirteen. After only six weeks—unless the rains last long enough for the birds to raise a second brood—the queleas are off again, following the end of the rains to a new region of abundance.

FEEDING STATIONS

In 1825, the English ornithologist John Freeman Dovaston set up an "ornithotrophe" outside his window. *Ornithotrophe* is Greek (sort of) for "bird feeder," and that snowy winter Dovaston's invention attracted twenty-three species of birds. Today, there are probably millions of bird feeders dispensing seeds, fruit, suet, or sugar water to birds over a good deal of the world.

Most people prefer to feed birds in winter. Once you start winter feeding, and birds get used to coming to your feeder to eat, you become responsible for making sure that your feeders are well supplied throughout the season. By offering food, you may be giving birds that would otherwise leave your area to find sources of natural food a reason to stay, and if you take that reason away in the middle of winter the birds that depend on you may starve. Once spring comes, there will be enough food for the birds without you, and many people stop supplying their feeders by the end of March.

You can, of course, keep your feeders going all year if you like. In spring or summer, you might want to switch from providing seeds to putting out sugar water for orioles or hummingbirds. Orioles will visit the plastic feeders designed to attract hummingbirds, or you can buy a special oriole feeder. You do not need to put food coloring in the water to convince the birds to come. Make sure that you do not use honey, which can be a source of infection. It is also very important to keep your oriole feeder scrupulously clean, because sugar water provides an excellent breeding ground for bacteria.

If you want to attract the widest possible range of birds to your garden, you should provide more than one type of feeder. Different species of birds have their own preferences. Some, like nuthatches, prefer suet stuffed in holes in a log or supplied in cakes in a special wire holder. Others—particularly small finches such as siskins and goldfinches—monopolize tube feeders with small entrance holes only their beaks can penetrate. These are particularly good for tiny seeds such as niger and millet. Even if a number of species prefer your main feeder, you may find that more aggressive birds will chase others away, and you may wish to provide a second feeder to give everyone a chance.

Cheap bird seed may not be a bargain. Birds have their likes and dislikes, and if you buy a mixed bag full of seeds that are not particularly popular with the birds, you may be paying a lot of money for nothing. You are better off learning what kind of seeds your birds like and spending a little more to get the right sorts. Scientists have studied which sorts of seeds backyard birds prefer, and find that the most popular are small black oil-type sunflower seeds and white proso millet. You can buy a number of specialized mixes at stores that specialize in bird-related supplies, including mixtures of already shelled seeds that, although they are more expensive, leave you with much less of a mess in your garden when the feeding season is over.

Birds will not be the only visitors to your feeder. A lot of your bounty will be grabbed by the local squirrels. They are particularly good at getting into almost any sort of feeder, although many dealers offer various sorts of squirrel guards or "squirrel-proof" feeders. You can even get squirrel-proof bird seed. This mixture is laced with cayenne pepper, which certainly gives the squirrels a surprise but does not seem to bother the birds at all. Some scientists have speculated that the chemicals that make peppers hot—known as capsaicins—may serve to keep rodents, which destroy the seeds, from eating the fruits of peppers without discouraging birds. The birds perform a service for the plant by digesting the fleshy part of the fruit but swallowing seeds whole, and carrying them away to be excreted with their droppings to grow into new plants somewhere else.

EIGHT

ON THE WING

Black of grackles glints purple as, wheeling in sun-glare,
The flock splays away to pepper the blueness of distance.
Soon they are lost in the tracklessness of air.
I watch them go. I stand in my trance.

Another year gone …

Grackles, goodbye! The sky will be vacant and lonely
Till again I hear your horde's rusty creak high above,
Confirming the year's turn and the fact that only, only,
In the name of Death do we learn the true name of Love.

—ROBERT PENN WARREN, *GRACKLES, GOODBYE*

The Bohemian Waxwing breeds in the northern forests of both the New and Old Worlds. It is an irruptive species, invading southern areas when there is not enough food in the north to sustain it.

Aristotle believed that swallows passed the winter hidden in holes or buried in mud. The truth is far stranger.

Every northern autumn, five billion birds migrate from North America to the West Indies, Central America, and South America, where the song of a Gray-cheeked Thrush may mingle with the cries of toucans and parrots. Five billion more leave Europe and Asia to journey to their wintering grounds in Africa, while birds from Japan and Siberia travel to Southeast Asia and the islands of Indonesia. Half a year later, a much smaller selection of birds—smaller, perhaps, because the lands themselves are so much smaller and milder in climate than their northern counterparts—fly north from southern South America, South Africa, and temperate Australia, seeking the Tropics.

Where a bird spends the winter may depend on tradition. The Northern Wheatear and the Yellow Wagtail are common Eurasian species that have established a foothold in North America. The North American birds, instead of migrating south to the American Tropics, fly back into Asia

Northern Wheatears have spread from Eurasia westward to Greenland and eastward to Alaska. Birds from the whole of this vast range winter in Africa, the New World birds crossing the ocean before turning south to follow their ancestral migration routes.

before heading south to winter with the rest of their species, in the Old World. Wheatears in Greenland cross 1,200 to 1,900 miles (2000–3000 km) of ocean to Britain to retrace their ancestral path into Africa. On the other hand, the North American Gray-cheeked Thrush has established a population in eastern Siberia that returns to North America every fall, before it, in turn, travels south.

Though the path of the Wheatear shows that migration can be a bird tradition, paradoxically it can also develop, or vanish, quite rapidly. In Europe, the Serin, a relative of the Canary once strictly resident around the Mediterranean, has spread north in the past hundred years, and the new arrivals in the North are migratory.

In January 1937, a flock of Fieldfares migrating across the North Sea from Norway to Britain was caught by a gale and blown westward. The birds were lucky enough to reach the southwestern corner of Greenland, where the great ice cap that covers most of the island gives way to stands of willow and birch scrub. Their descendants are there still, but no longer as migrants. They have become year-round residents.

Migration may be as old as the long treks the dinosaurs made between their breeding and wintering grounds. But the routes songbirds follow today may be no older than the last ice age. Eighteen thousand years ago, much of the world lay buried under tons of ice. Birds had no choice but to stay in the lower latitudes. As the ice sheets retreated, birds followed them north and south to newly green lands. Today, their descendants retrace those journeys, their paths defining the great migration systems of the world.

The Fieldfare is a common winter visitor to western Europe, where it often feeds on fallen apples. In the 1930s, a migrating flock of Fieldfares was driven by Atlantic storms westward to Greenland, where they remained and gave up their migratory habits.

One hundred sixty-four songbird species migrate from temperate North America south into the New World Tropics. They include fifty warblers, thirty-one flycatchers, and thirteen orioles and blackbirds. Other species do not reach the Tropics at all, wintering instead in the southern United States, or, like Snow Buntings, among the snowy fields of southern Canada or New England.

From the East, North American migrants fly to the West Indies, or across the Caribbean to Central or South America. From the West, they funnel into the pine forests of Mexico, or follow the land mass of Central America farther south. Migrating birds triple the number of species on Grand Bahama every winter. On Barro Colorado Island in the Panama Canal, one of every sixteen birds is a migrant. In October, at the peak of migration, the number goes up to one in seven.

The Wrenlike Rushbird is a South American ovenbird that looks, and acts, like a North American Marsh Wren. It is an austral migrant, breeding in southern South American marshes and wintering farther north.

One hundred forty-one temperate South American passerine species migrate to the North. More than half are tyrant flycatchers: long-legged, short-tailed ground-tyrants; greenish, short-billed elaenias; sleek and graceful black-tyrants; Austral Negritos; Chocolate-vented Tyrants; Crowned Slaty-Flycatchers. Wrenlike Rushbirds, White-tipped Plantcutters, Chilean Swallows, Common Diuca-Finches, Pampas Meadowlarks, and others fill out the remainder.

Most of these austral migrants live in open country—unlike North American migrants, which tend to be forest birds. Only one of the sixteen songbirds of the southern beech forests of Argentina and Chile, the White-crested Elaenia, leaves for the winter.

The Vermilion Flycatcher straddles both American migration systems. Birds from the southwestern United States winter in Mexico or Central America (a few end up in south Florida). Vermilion Flycatchers in the Tropics stay put. There is even a resident population in the Galápagos that rides about on the backs of giant tortoises. Still farther south they are migratory again, flying north from Argentina and Chile to escape the austral winter.

Across the Atlantic, more than two hundred species of birds take part in the great migration system flowing from Eurasia into Africa. Almost one-fifth of the migrants are Willow Warblers, some from as far away as Siberia.

European birds on their way to winter in Africa usually cross the Mediterranean and the Sahara in one long flight, a distance of more than 1,800 miles (3000 km). In the spring, migrating birds must wait out head winds that may blow south across the Sahara or they will be unable to complete their northward journey.

Few Eurasian songbirds risk flying over the deserts of central Asia and the heights of the Himalayas to winter in India. Many more species—pipits, starlings, shrikes, flycatchers,

thrushes, buntings—follow a far eastern route to Southeast Asia or—for a few Yellow Wagtails and Barn Swallows—northern Australia.

Some South African birds—Black Saw-wing Swallows, African Paradise-Flycatchers, and others—migrate north and east from the Cape to Natal. Though African Cliff Swallows travel to western Zaïre, a distance of some 1,500 miles (2400 km), only about twenty species from southern Africa winter as far north as the Tropics. A number of tropical African species travel back and forth across the equator as the seasons change from wet to dry. They include larks, a few warblers, some swallows, and the African Pitta.

Australia has any number of birds that wander about the continent, following the shifting patterns of rain and droughts, but comparatively few regular migrants. Among them are White-winged Trillers, Satin Flycatchers, Black-faced Monarchs, and several honeyeaters, such as the Yellow-faced Honeyeater and the Noisy Friarbird. Many only travel within the continent, or

Vermilion Flycatchers migrate southward from southern North America and northward from southern South America, but this bird, from the Galápagos Islands, stays at home, where it occasionally hitches a ride on the back of a giant tortoise.

The distinctive Gurney's Sugarbird is found only in the mountains of southern Africa, where it migrates altitudinally, seeking lower elevations in the austral winter.

Not every migrant flies from north to south, or from south to north. Chaffinches from Scandinavia fly westward to winter in Britain. In the Alps, Chaffinches fly not south or west but downhill, from higher in the mountains, where they breed, to lower elevations.

Altitudinal migration, quite common among mountain birds, is a far less costly and dangerous way of getting to a winter home than is a long-distance flight. On the Atlantic slope of Costa Rica, White-ruffed Manakins breed in wet forests at about 1,800 feet (550 m) elevation, but may leave the area in the autumn for wintering grounds lower down the mountain slopes. At least seventy-six species of birds are altitudinal migrants in the mountainous province of Kwazulu-Natal in South Africa. They include swallows, thrushes, warblers, flycatchers, pipits, finches, and strange South African specialties such as the Orange-breasted Rock-Jumper and Gurney's Sugarbird.

Many songbirds migrate at night. This may seem odd, but there are good reasons for it. The air is usually less turbulent, making for better flying conditions, and cooler, making for lower heat and water loss. There are fewer predators about waiting to pick off migrants on the wing (hawks migrate by day, when soaring conditions are better). Finally, a bird may need the daylight hours to find more food to fuel it for its onward journey. This is not a problem for swallows, which feed on the wing anyway and migrate by day, as do most finches, crows, jays, buntings, and wagtails.

Birds that fly nonstop for large parts of their journey may fly by both night and day. That is true for Blackpoll Warblers and other American songbirds that fly from New England to South America over the Atlantic. In Europe, the Sedge Warbler may fly 1,900 miles (3000 km) in one nonstop flight that may take three or four days.

Songbirds are not particularly high fliers as migrating birds go. Radar studies show that on the average, half of them fly below 1,300 to 2,300 feet (400–700 m), and 90 percent of them below 5,000 to 6,600 feet (1500–2000 m). The record height for songbirds studied this way is about 19,700 feet (6000 m), but this is usually rare.

Migrating songbirds may fly very low indeed. In the autumn of 1975, observers at Falsterbo in southern Sweden recorded some fifteen thousand Coal Tits migrating out over the sea at an altitude of a foot or so. Thrushes flying to Britain in fall do not get picked up on radar until it is nearly dawn. It seems that the birds fly very low during the night, but climb rapidly as the sun rises and they near land. Flying low may help them avoid strong tail winds that could blow them right past the British Isles into the open Atlantic, almost certainly to their deaths.

Why do migrating birds put themselves through this difficult and costly ordeal? The answer to this question, for once, is quite straightforward: they migrate to find food. Climate has little to do with it, at least not directly. Birds will remain in the North through the harshest winters if food is available, as anyone who runs a bird feeder knows. Birds that live on seeds, or that can find wintering insects beneath the bark of trees, do not need to migrate. Some insect-eating birds, like the Bearded Reedling of Europe, can avoid being forced to migrate by shifting their winter diet from insects to seeds.

But a bird that catches flying insects, or plucks them from deciduous leaves, or eats fruit or nectar, must leave the North (or the Far South) if it is to survive. In Europe, Spotted and Pied Flycatchers both feed on flying insects. The Pied Flycatcher, though, can also snap them up from the ground. This difference lets the Pied return to its breeding grounds at least three weeks earlier than the Spotted, before large numbers of flying insects become available.

Why do birds that live on foods like these bother to live in the Temperate Zone at all? Why not just stay in the Tropics, as so many birds do?

The Temperate Zone offers considerable advantages for a bird that can reach it—long days, abundant insect food (I have never been in a tropical rainforest whose mosquito population came close to what I have suffered in an Ontario woodland in June), and far fewer competitors. Seen in this way, a Scarlet Tanager in Canada, or a Fairy Pitta in Japan, is really a tropical bird that has moved north, away from the vast majority of its relatives, who never leave the Tropics.

The need to migrate shapes a bird's body and drives much of its metabolism. Short, broad wings are excellent for maneuvering in brush or thick vegetation, but long, pointed wings are better for long-distance flying. So we find that in European marshes Cetti's Warbler, a resident, has a rounded wing, while the wing of the migrant Reed Warbler is long and narrow. In Brazil, migratory Variegated Flycatchers have longer and narrower wings than do resident birds living in the northern part of their range, close to the equator.

Food—or, rather, the lack of it—is also the driving force behind the movements of some birds that are not regular migrants. When seed crops in the northern coniferous forests are low, birds that depend on those seeds may make mass flights to other climes. These journeys are called *irruptions*. Irruptive species include Bohemian Waxwings, crossbills, Pine Grosbeaks, and Eurasian Nutcrackers. Failures in the locust population may force Rosy Starlings to irrupt from the steppes of central Asia. In Australia, Masked and Black-faced Woodswallows wander from the dry interior to coastal areas, especially during harsh years.

If a returning migrant can make it back to its breeding grounds ahead of its fellows, it may have first choice of the finest territories or the fittest mates. It may also run the risk of a late winter storm or no food to eat when it arrives. Birds get around this problem, if it happens, by *reverse migration*—turning around and heading back south. Some of the busiest spring days at Point Pelee, Ontario, occur when the birds, attempting to fly north, hit a cold front at the base of the point and head back south again.

Of course, it is better for the birds if they do not hit bad weather conditions. To avoid them, birds will not fly north if the atmospheric pressure is low, a sign of an oncoming storm. They prefer the clear weather brought on by a high-pressure system, and a clear starry sky on a spring night is an invitation for them to make the best of their flying time to the North, often skipping over the resting spots where chagrined birders await them.

Migration, like so many other aspects of a bird's life, depends on timing, and a migrant's internal clock can be remarkably accurate. The return of Cliff Swallows to the mission of San Juan

Capistrano in California every March 19 (or close to it) is fabled in song, tourist brochure, and Web site (http://www.sanjuancapistrano.com:80/MissionSJC/mission3.html).

The internal clock, though, does have some flexibility. Weather does not always observe the calendar. An American Robin can fine-tune its departure to avoid plunging into a late storm or a blizzard. The clock may be set differently for males and females. Male Red-winged Blackbirds arrive in the North anywhere from one to five weeks ahead of the females, to stake out their territories before potential mates arrive. So do Skylarks.

The first sign that a songbird's internal clock is beginning to set off the migration alarm has been known to cage-bird fanciers for two centuries. As the time for departure draws near, a caged songbird may awaken shortly after dark and flutter for hours at the bars of its cage. This restlessness is called, in German, *Zugunruhe*, and it is set off by changes in day length. As days grow longer or shorter, depending on the season, migratory birds grow more restless and begin to overeat, building up their fat reserves for the journey.

Zugunruhe is not just a feature of northern migrants. Silvereyes from Tasmania and southern Australia show it, too, as they prepare to migrate northward to their wintering grounds and again in the autumn before they return to the South.

The fuel for a migrating bird's flight lies under its skin, in the form of thick layers of fat. Every gram of fat burned yields more than twice the energy of a gram of carbohydrate or protein. Unlike carbohydrates, fat can be stored without taking on extra water. Even a bird whose body is only 10 percent fat can fly on the strength of it for ten to twenty hours, enough to cross 300 miles (500 km) in still weather. Portable and efficient, fat is the ideal fuel.

A long-distance migrant needs to gain enough fat to amount to about 40 percent of its body weight, enough to carry it about 1,550 miles (2500 km). Short-range migrants, with no oceans to cross, need to be only about 20 percent fat at the beginning of migration—still well above the 3 to 5 percent figure for nonmigrants. Putting on that fat means a frenzy of feeding before the journey begins.

The Silvereye is not only a regular migrant in Australia, but is also a considerable traveler. In the last century, it established itself in New Zealand, where this bird is feeding on an autumn crop of poro-poro fruit.

The amount of fat a migrating bird needs to take on before setting out may depend on how good its chances are of refueling en route. Songbirds that migrate over land often stop every sixty miles (100 km) or so to take on more food and replenish their fat reserves—if they can. Barn Swallows and Red-backed Shrikes need less fat to cross the Sahara than do Whitethroats and Garden Warblers, because the swallows can find flying insects over the desert and the shrikes can eat the other migrants. The warblers have no such chance, and must have enough food reserves to cross the whole of the desert if they are to survive their journey south. To gain as much weight as possible, Red-Eyed Vireos, Hermit Thrushes, and many other American birds switch their diet from insects to berries, deliberately seeking out berry-rich refueling sites.

Fattening up is so important that if Spotted Flycatchers run out of fat reserves in midtravel, they can turn off their migratory urges until they have time to refuel. A really lean Spotted

Some Blue Jays in the Toronto region stay in the city all year. Others migrate through the city in large numbers. In the autumn, several thousand may fly out over Lake Ontario in a single day.

Flycatcher may stop at an oasis in the Sahara for almost a month to build up its supply of fat, before heading off again to its real wintering grounds.

When Blackpoll Warblers arrive on the coast of Massachusetts in September, they have almost no fat reserves. They cannot refuel on their transatlantic flight, so they cannot leave until they practically double their weight, from around a half ounce (12 g) to almost one ounce (20 g). This can take them three weeks or more. They do not eat continuously, but wait to put on the last few tenths of an ounce until they sense the approach of a cold front. That way, they can be sure of a full tank of fuel when the northwest winds following the front arrive to help them on their way.

Even a bird that is half fat cannot travel far without a well-tuned metabolism. The Blackpoll Warbler fuels its Atlantic trek by burning body fat so efficiently—losing about 0.6 percent of its body weight per hour of flight, compared with about 1 percent for most songbirds—that it gets the equivalent of 720,000 miles per gallon (250 000 km/l). Efficient or not, it loses almost all of its fat, burned off to fuel the trip, before it arrives in South America.

All the preparation in the world would make no difference to migrating birds if they did not have some way to tell where they were going once they set off. Migrating birds have a remarkable ability to navigate, even under unusual circumstances. Richard Mewaldt trapped White-crowned Sparrows on their wintering grounds in San Jose, California, and flew them to Baton Rouge, Louisiana. The next winter, the birds were back in California. Dr. Mewaldt flew them to Laurel, Maryland. Once again, they returned, perhaps by way of their breeding grounds in Alaska.

European Starlings can navigate by the sun. Not only can they orient to the sun's position in the sky, but they can compensate for that position as it changes throughout the day. Night

There are dozens of species of tanagers in the New World Tropics, but the brilliant Scarlet Tanager is the only one that breeds regularly in southeastern Canada. Is it a northern bird that winters in the Tropics, or a tropical bird that breeds in the north?

migrants steer by the stars. Ornithologist Stephen Emlen showed that Indigo Buntings could orient by constellations such as the Big Dipper or Draco. If clouds blocked one constellation, the birds could still line themselves up properly using the others. The birds do not find north, as you might expect, by homing in on the Pole Star. Instead, they can sense the rotation of the stars through the sky as the night progresses, and find north by steering for the center of the rotation—a point that shifts as the earth spins through the 26,000-year cycle of the procession of the equinoxes. As the birds have evolved, their orientation has shifted with the earth. They could always find true north, wherever the pole pointed.

Birds navigate properly even on overcast nights. It turns out that they have yet another built-in compass, this one oriented, like a real compass, to the earth's magnetic field. So, by the way, do many other animals—including, to a limited extent, human beings, though we are seldom aware of it.

Despite all the built-in safeguards that keep birds on their course, sometimes the system fails badly. The result is a bird that ends up hundreds, or even thousands, of miles from where it is supposed to be. A bird out of range is called an *accidental*, the stuff of telephoned rare-bird alerts and excited messages passed back and forth between birders. Some of these birds have been caught by storms. Westerlies blowing across the Atlantic have dropped many North American songbirds in the British Isles.

Sometimes, though, it seems that accidentals have strayed because of a defect in their navigation system. Often, these are young birds, probably on their first migration, and for some reason have set off in the wrong direction. That may explain Asian warblers in the Shetland Islands, the Siberian Rubythroat found on the grill of a car in Ontario, or the Variegated Flycatcher—a bird from Argentina and Brazil—that survived for a few cold November weeks on Toronto Island. Exciting as their appearance is to birders, such birds are almost certainly doomed.

The orientation system of night-flying migrants has one serious, and often fatal, flaw: an inability to adjust for the lights that flicker from buildings, monuments, or lighthouses. Particularly on overcast nights, hundreds, even thousands, of birds may fly into these beams of man-made light, either crashing into the building walls or, after fluttering exhausted in the beam, falling to the ground. On September 20, 1957, some twenty thousand birds, mostly warblers, thrushes, and tanagers, were killed at a single thousand-foot (300 m) TV tower in Eau Claire, Wisconsin. In many cities, the owners of office buildings have been persuaded to turn down their lights during the peak days of migration.

The ability to orient is not simply hard-wired into bird brains at birth. Some of it must be learned. If baby Indigo Buntings cannot see the night sky regularly during their first month of life, they can use the earth's magnetic field, but are unable to steer by the stars. European Starlings nest in holes in trees, so their nestlings cannot see the sky. Young starlings must learn by experience. It may take them almost a year— well after their first fall migration—to learn to steer by the sun. In a famous experiment, A. C. Perdeck flew more than eleven thousand starlings, over a ten-year period, from Holland to Switzerland. The adult birds were able, somehow, to figure out where they were, adjust their flight paths accordingly, and fly to their usual wintering grounds. The young birds could not make this adjustment, took off in what would have been the proper direction were they still in Holland, and ended up in the wrong place.

This Variegated Flycatcher, photographed on Toronto Island in southern Ontario in November, is thousands of miles from its home in southern Brazil and northern Argentina. It aroused great excitement among North American birders, but almost certainly at the cost of its own life.

It appears, then, that birds are hatched with one kind of compass—the one that orients to the earth's magnetic field—and learn to add celestial compasses relying on the sun and the stars. The older they get, the more they can fine-tune their migration using a variety of different cues: familiar landmarks, perhaps even familiar smells. European Starlings deprived of their sense of smell were much less able to find their way home over long distances than birds left intact.

Birds may use other clues, too: more arcane phenomena such as gravitational and Coriolis forces. We do not yet understand the full range of these clues, or how the birds integrate them. We can only marvel—as we must at the whole of migration—that they can do it at all.

FROM BIRDING TO ORNITHOLOGY

Margaret Morse Nice was a housewife who watched Song Sparrows from her home in Ohio. She was not a professional ornithologist—but in 1943 she published a 328-page paper, "Studies in the life history of the Song Sparrow," that has become a scientific classic and is still almost unmatched in its knowledge and detail. When it comes to the study of birds, amateurs can make a real contribution.

Birding, according to some people, is just a sport. Feeding birds in your backyard is recreation. But if you enjoy either or both of these things, for a little extra care and effort you can make a real contribution to science. One way to do this is to join one of several projects designed to allow you to collect information about birds and contribute it to a central database, where the information can be pooled and studied to tell us things about where birds live, where they travel, and how their populations are changing.

The oldest of these efforts—perhaps the oldest wildlife population study in the world—is the Christmas Bird Count, sponsored by the National Audubon Society. Christmas Bird Counts have been held every year since 1900. Today, birders all over North America, and in a few other places, as well, conduct more than fifteen hundred Christmas Bird Counts. There will almost certainly be one in or near your area, and its organizers will be glad to welcome you to the fold. Christmas Counts are not necessarily (in fact, not usually) held on Christmas Day, so participating in one should not interrupt your holiday activities.

Christmas Bird Counts are not the only surveys you can join. Your local naturalists' organization should be able to alert you to breeding-bird surveys, roadside censuses, or atlasing projects designed to map the distribution of breeding birds throughout your province or state. The American Birding Association publishes an annual directory of volunteer opportunities for birders in their magazine *On Wings*. I have included their address at the back of this book.

The Cornell Laboratory of Ornithology has begun a series of valuable and interesting projects as part of their Citizen Science program. You don't even have to leave home to be part of one of their most popular studies, Project FeederWatch, a joint program of Cornell and the Long Point Bird Observatory in Ontario. All you have to do is spend a little time (or as much as you like) counting the birds that come to your feeder in winter, and sending in the results each spring. The information the project has gathered gives us an invaluable picture of population changes from place to place and from year to year—a picture that becomes increasingly important as we become more and more concerned about the effect that environmental change has on all of us. Bird populations may provide us with one of the best indicators of those changes, so the information from studies such as Project FeederWatch has a value far beyond ornithological curiosity.

More than ten thousand people in the United States and two thousand people in Canada have joined Project FeederWatch, and the information from it has already been used to study changes in the populations and movements of Common Redpolls and Varied Thrushes. Project FeederWatch members have also taken part in a study of eye infections that have been spreading through the House Finch population in eastern North America since they were first noticed in Maryland in 1993. The House Finch Disease Survey has already collected more than eighteen thousand data forms.

In 1998, Cornell will launch a special extension of the program for middle schools. Classroom FeederWatch teaches students about bird identification and biology, and allows them to share their findings with other classrooms over the Internet. If you are on the Internet yourself, you can find out about this project, and other Citizen Science projects such as the Cornell Nest Box Network, at http://www.tc.cornell.edu/Birds.

NINE

MINESHAFT CANARIES

There is special providence in the fall of a sparrow.

—WILLIAM SHAKESPEARE, *HAMLET*

In the late 1950s, Chairman Mao Zedong proclaimed the Eurasian Tree Sparrow (which, in the Far East, is the sparrow of towns and cities) to be an Enemy of the State.

Chinese newspapers announced that "Each sparrow eats on average 7 catties (1 catty = 0.67 kg) of grain per year. Fifty million sparrows will thus eat as much as will feed three million people per year." Every citizen was drafted into a sparrow war, destroying nests, poisoning and shooting the birds, or catching them with bird lime. Those too old to participate banged gongs and tins, set off firecrackers, and waved flags, keeping the birds away from their roosts until the birds dropped from exhaustion.

The war lasted three days and killed millions of sparrows. Nearly a million died in Beijing alone. In the years that followed, grain production fell as hordes of insect pests the sparrows would have eaten invaded the victors' fields and reaped their harvest.

For all the pleasure and benefit songbirds have given us, our relations with them have often been no more friendly, and no more intelligent, than that. Millions of American blackbirds have been killed in the name of control of the fungal disease histoplasmosis, though the birds

apparently have little to do with its spread to humans. Clearing away vegetation to destroy blackbird roosts may actually help spread the infection, by exposing the bare soil where the fungal spores really lie.

We have, for no good reason, redesigned the songbird landscape around us. As Western civilization advanced across the globe, its pioneers brought European birds with them to replace the natives of their new lands. The international bird trade reversed the process, importing birds from the far corners of the world.

New Zealand, a land of birds if ever there was one, could not satisfy Europeans with its Tuis, New Zealand Bellbirds, and kiwis. They were not English enough, and in an effort to bring a taste of home to the Antipodes, naturalization societies released at least eighty-nine species of birds in the islands. Today, New Zealand's commonest songbirds are sparrows and finches, species brought from England before the turn of the century.

"We need more songsters here," bemoaned the Honolulu *Commercial Advertiser* in August 1860. More than 150 species of birds from around the world were brought to the

Hawaiian Islands by societies such as the Hui Manu, organized specifically for that purpose in 1930. The birds carried more with them than their songs. Avian malaria and avian pox, diseases unknown in the islands, swept through Hawaii's native birds as high into the mountains as the mosquitoes that carry them could reach. They may have delivered the final blow to the oos and Hawaiian honeycreepers that survived the destruction of their forests and the introduction of the mongoose and the rat.

The House Sparrow was first brought to North America in 1850, to control cankerworms. The European Starling was released in Central Park, New York City, in 1890 by a group that planned to introduce all the birds mentioned by Shakespeare. You can find it in *Henry IV, Part I*, and today practically throughout the continent—not to mention in Australia, New Zealand, South Africa, Jamaica, Hawaii, Fiji, Tonga. In North America, the sparrow and the starling have been blamed for the decline of the Eastern Bluebird, which they evict from its cavity nests.

Our zeal to change the biological landscape around us reaches a sort of zenith in South Miami, Florida, where introduced Red-whiskered Bulbuls eat the berries of introduced plants, nest in introduced trees among gardens full of introduced lizards and frogs, their songs occasionally drowned out by the shriek of introduced parrots flying over canals where introduced fishes swim. This host of alien animals is mostly there by accident, escapees from the international pet trade.

Birds have been kept as pets for centuries. In Asia, "prayer birds" are sold to be released as part of a Buddhist requirement to perform good deeds. In the West, the Canary has been domesticated for generations, and now bears little resemblance to its drab wild ancestor. But millions of wild songbirds are still trapped every year to be sold as cage birds.

The United States used to be the largest market for wild birds in the world, importing more than two million birds from eighty-five countries between 1986 and 1988 alone. More than half of them—54 percent—were small finches, mostly from Africa, and for every one that reached a pet store perhaps ten died en route.

(opposite) The Straw-headed Bulbul of Southeast Asia is a victim of its own singing ability. A popular cage bird in Asia, it has been trapped in large numbers and is now rare in many parts of its range.

I was in Dakar, Senegal, in August 1966:

We visited a place where finches, mist-netted or snared, are brought in for export to Europe as cagebirds… Thousands of birds are crammed into cages they can hardly move in; others, far too many for a cage, fly about in the smelly rooms, destroying and shedding their plumage. The Paradise-Whydahs, especially, were a sickening sight. Sick, dying and dead birds are everywhere, and the keepers tread on many… I only wish I had had a pair of wire clippers or an axe.

The bird trade still goes on, though since 1975 it has been partly regulated by the Convention on International Trade in Endangered Species of Wild Fauna and Flora (CITES). CITES, however, applies only to species listed on its Appendices. The list of CITES songbirds is fairly short. Ghana has placed many of its finches on Appendix III, which allows CITES to regulate trade in birds coming from that country, but none of the African finches is listed on Appendix I or II, which would either ban them from international commercial trade (Appendix I) or regulate them throughout their range (Appendix II).

The global trade in wild songbirds is wasteful and destructive, but it threatens relatively few songbirds—compared with, say, parrots—with imminent extinction. Trade certainly has endangered the Red Siskin of Venezuela, heavily trapped to breed "red factor" Canaries. Cage-bird poachers have reduced the Bali Myna, a beautiful white, lacy-crested creature, to fewer than fifty wild birds, though hundreds survive in captivity. Even the well-known Java Sparrow is in trouble in the wild. The victim of years of intense trapping and persecution from rice farmers—at least twenty thousand birds a year were shipped from Java and Bali in the early nineties, six thousand for release at a single wedding in Singapore—this once-common species is in serious decline.

Canada, the United States, and many other countries ban the export of their wild birds. Australia banned imports and exports of wildlife in 1960. In 1992, the United States passed the

Wild Bird Conservation Act (WBCA), which bans import of CITES-listed species, except for personal pets, research, and approved breeding programs. Since its passage, the number of birds imported to the U.S. has fallen from an average of seven hundred thousand per year during the 1980s to fewer than one hundred thousand in 1994. Today, the American pet trade is beginning to rely more on captive-bred birds, and many aviculturists are distancing themselves from the trappers and importers.

Huge numbers of seedeaters, siskins, and other songbirds, though, are still trapped for local sale in Brazil and Argentina. Some, like the Yellow Cardinal, have already become rare. An undercover investigator I met in Brazil in 1991 told me about a single dealer who was receiving three hundred Red-crested Cardinals a week. In Southeast Asia, at least five hundred species of birds *not* listed on CITES are traded locally with little or no regulation or control, including rare and little-known birds that are supposed to be fully protected. At least one species, the Straw-headed Bulbul, has been almost wiped out by trappers in Indonesia. The bird is prized for its song, and is now being imported from Malaysia to meet Indonesian demand. It was proposed for CITES listing in 1997.

Some thirty species of songbirds have disappeared in the past four hundred years, almost all of them confined to oceanic islands. When humans arrived, accompanied by their pigs, dogs, cats, rats, and diseases, island birds had either nowhere to hide or, having evolved without predators, no instinct to try. The only recent songbirds we know whose extinction unquestionably had nothing to do with humankind were the San Benedicto race of the Rock Wren, whose habitat was destroyed by a volcanic eruption in 1952, and the St. Kitts race of the Puerto Rican Bullfinch, which apparently disappeared after two hurricanes swept the island in 1899.

New Zealand has lost the Bush and Stephens Island Wrens, the Huia, and the Piopio, the so-called New Zealand "thrush" that may have been a primitive bowerbird. Lord Howe Island, a mountainous fragment lying three hundred miles (480 km) east of Australia, lost the Lord Howe (this page and opposite) Fuzzy images of vanished birds are almost all we have left to tell us what the Bachman's Warbler (right), Guam Flycatcher(far right), and Kauai Oo (opposite) were like. The flycatcher literally disappeared down the throat of brown tree snakes accidentally released on Guam. The Kauai Oo may have fallen victim to exotic diseases. Bachman's Warbler may have suffered a double blow: the loss of the forest where it bred and the almost complete conversion of its Cuban wintering habitat to sugar cane farms.

Island White-eye, and three distinctive races of other songbirds, when large numbers of rats came ashore from a ship beached in 1918 to save her from sinking.

In a more recent, and devastating, tragedy, populations of every native songbird on Guam declined catastrophically in the seventies and eighties. The Guam Flycatcher and the local races of Rufous Fantail and Bridled White-eye have vanished entirely, and all the rest are in serious danger. The few survivors linger in a narrow strip of forest at Ritidian Point below the island's northern cliffs. To the astonishment (and, indeed, initial disbelief) of scientists, it seems that there is only one culprit: the Brown Tree Snake (*Boiga irregularis*), accidentally introduced from Manus Island near New Guinea in the aftermath of World War II. The snakes, after reaching densities of probably twelve thousand per square mile, ate almost every songbird on Guam.

The greatest songbird holocaust in history, though, took place on Hawaii. The early Polynesians, who arrived in the islands sometime between A.D. 200 and 500, converted much of the lowland forest into taro fields and introduced pigs, dogs, and the Pacific Rat. At least twenty songbirds, including seventeen Hawaiian honeycreepers, two crows, and a honeyeater, disappeared sometime after their arrival. The existence of these songbirds was not even suspected by scientists until their sub-fossil bones turned up in the 1970s.

By the time Captain Cook "discovered" the islands in 1778, forty-two songbirds survived: the Hawaiian Crow, the Elepaio and Millerbird, five thrushes, five honeyeaters, and twenty-nine Hawaiian honeycreepers. They soon began to vanish in their turn. Some, like the Kioea and the Oahu Oo, disappeared in the early nineteenth century, but most of the rest underwent their

sharpest decline in the early years of the twentieth. One thrush, four honeyeaters, and nine Hawaiian honeycreepers are now extinct, and the crow, three thrushes, the one (possibly) surviving honeyeater, and ten honeycreepers are listed as Critical or Endangered. The Hawaii Oos and Mamos, whose feathers decorated the cloak of King Kamehameha, are gone. The remnants of Hawaii's native songbirds cling to life in the remote forests of the highlands.

Today, wild habitats on the continents may themselves be no more than islands in a sea of human settlements and cultivation. Many songbirds, particularly birds of the interior of tropical forests, cannot cross that sea. As their habitats shrink and degrade, more and more are joining the Hawaiian survivors on the endangered list. The 1996 Red List of Threatened Animals, published by the World Conservation Union (IUCN), lists 72 passerine species as Critical, 114 as Endangered, and 356 as Vulnerable.

There have, it is true, been some returns from the dead—though the returnees are critically rare. In 1996, the Kinglet Calyptura, smallest of the cotingas, turned up alive only thirty-

The Seychelles Magpie-Robin was once the world's rarest songbird, reduced to fewer than ten birds on a single islet in the Seychelles. Though its numbers are slightly higher now, and it has been relocated to two other islands, it is still one of the most critically endangered birds in the world.

eight miles (60 km) from Rio de Janeiro after an absence of almost 150 years. The São Tomé Grosbeak was rediscovered in August 1991 after having gone missing since 1890. The Cebu Flowerpecker, unseen since 1906, reappeared in 1992 in a tiny patch of Philippine forest that could disappear within five years. Its only hope may be an education program for the people of the nearby village of Tabunan, who will determine whether the trees it lives in will end up as bird habitat or timber.

The Noisy Scrub-Bird was thought to have been extinct since 1889 until between forty and forty-five pairs were rediscovered in 1961 at Two Peoples Bay, a popular recreation spot near Albany in southwestern Australia. Thanks to wildfire prevention, translocation, and the work of volunteers who census the singing males of this notoriously shy bird (saving the

Australian government more than A\$100,000 a year in the process), there are now five separate populations of Noisy Scrub-Birds with more than three hundred singing males.

For the rest, except for the birds that we persecute or capture directly, the chief threat to their existence is the loss or degradation of their habitats. In a few cases, disease may be a factor. The Gouldian Finch, common as a cage bird but in decline in the wild, may be infested with air-sac mites. Sometimes there are so many in a finch's windpipe that it has difficulty breathing.

The Noisy Scrub-Bird of Southwestern Australia was once thought to be extinct. Since its rediscovery it has been the subject of an intense and largely successful conservation program, with active participation by Australian birders.

Some birds need intense, continuous, hands-on conservation. The Seychelles Magpie-Robin was once found on at least seven islands in the Seychelles. By 1959, introduced cats and rats had reduced it to twenty individuals on a single, tiny rat-free island, Fregate. By 1965, there were only twelve. Conservationists eliminated cats on Fregate, and by 1978, numbers had grown slowly (the bird lays only one egg per clutch) to forty-one. Unfortunately, the robins depended on coconut plantations, where they could feed in workers' gardens and on the mown lawns beneath the palm trees. In 1982, coconut growing was virtually abandoned on Fregate. The workers left, undergrowth encroached on the plantations, and, by 1990, the robin population was back to about twenty.

The International Council for Bird Preservation (now Birdlife International), working with the Seychelles government and the owner of Fregate, set up a recovery program for the species. Workers planted more trees on the island, provided nest boxes, put out extra food, and in 1992 and 1994 translocated birds to neighboring Cousin, Cousine, and Aride. By the end of 1995, there were sixty Magpie-Robins on the various islands, the highest number for years. In the same year, though, brown rats got loose on Fregate, and the recovery team has had to start another program to control them. And so it goes.

Even the best efforts may fail. The Dusky Seaside Sparrow was a strikingly marked, noisy bird that had the misfortune to be confined to a small area in and around Merritt Island on the east coast of Florida. Its salt-marsh home was subjected to everything from flooding for mosquito control to the construction of the Kennedy Space Center. Two years after Brian Sharp discovered the largest known colony in 1968, the Florida State Department of Transportation drove an expressway through it.

The last female disappeared in 1977. Biologists trapped the five surviving males in 1980, intending to crossbreed them with Seaside Sparrows from the Gulf Coast. Their next step would have been to mate offspring from the crosses to the Duskies again, in the hope that eventually nearly pure birds would result—a technique called *backcrossing*. The U.S. Fish and Wildlife Service, however, refused to support the program, on the grounds that it might violate the U.S. Endangered Species Act and would not be worth the money—the bird was doomed anyway. The last pure Dusky, a bird named Orange, died at the age of twelve on June 12, 1987. The few hybrids that had been bred died under mysterious circumstances two years later.

Trying to save the world's songbirds species by species will not work. Even on a single-species basis, waiting until a bird is in crisis before acting guarantees that our efforts will be expensive, difficult, and risky. That is not to say such efforts are not worth making—I would not let a single species vanish without a fight. But there are more effective ways to protect the birds of the world from our conscious and unconscious depredations. The key—except for those species suffering from direct persecution—is not just to protect the birds, but to preserve their habitat, and to do it before they join the endangered list.

We may finally be waking up to this in North America. We have few critically endangered birds here, but in recent years birders, scientists, and the caring public have grown more and more concerned about a broader problem: is something happening to our migrating songbirds?

For many years, migrants flying over a weather station at Lake Charles, Louisiana, have been picked up on the station's radar. When Sidney Gauthreaux analyzed the radar data, he found that migrating birds showed up on 50 percent fewer spring nights in 1987–89 than in 1965–67. Gauthreaux's findings alarmed many scientists, but they just might mean that the same number of birds are traveling in larger groups on fewer days. Other evidence, though, suggests that the birds themselves are vanishing. On islands off the coast of Maryland, for example, migrant songbirds are only half as numerous as they were in the 1940s. Kentucky and Hooded Warblers have disappeared altogether, and Red-eyed Vireos and Ovenbirds have declined by at least 70 percent.

What is going on? Some have suggested that the birds are suffering from the loss of their winter homes. There is no question that habitat destruction in the New World Tropics is a serious ecological problem. But does it really affect our migrating songbirds?

We are still not sure. The destruction of tropical lowland rainforest is not as great a threat for migrants as it is for the birds that live there year-round. Relatively few of our songbirds winter in the Amazon, for instance. Less than 30 percent use humid forests anywhere as their primary winter home. The others winter in second growth, scrubland, dry forest, and other habitats. Northern migrants are rarely confined to a single habitat in winter, so that the destruction of one type of tropical forest or scrubland would be unlikely to devastate them. Many northern migrants winter widely in tropical America, giving them extra insurance should one region be particularly hard hit. Only twenty-one species are confined to a single region.

The most important parts of South America for northern migrants are the forests at middle elevations in the northern and central Andes. Here, Canada Warblers, Scarlet Tanagers, and Olive-sided Flycatchers winter in primary forests that are rapidly being logged and replaced with crops of coffee, cacao, and coca.

Far more important than the Amazon—and equally at risk—are the forests of Central America and the West Indies. Not only do many of our birds winter there, but they may be so densely packed into their winter woodlands that the loss of a single acre (0.4 ha) in Mexico or the

Dominican Republic may affect five times as many birds as the loss of an acre of their breeding territories in the North. Eighty-six species, mostly from western North America, winter in the pine and pine-oak woodlands of Mexico and northern Central America. Bicknell's Thrush, a bird of the mountain forests of New England that until only recently was considered to be a race of the more widespread Gray-cheeked Thrush, winters (as far as we know) solely on the island of Hispaniola. Hispaniolan forests are disappearing or, on the Haitian side of the island, have pretty much disappeared already.

Migrants are under pressure, though, at both ends of their range, and it is very difficult to determine which end is doing the most damage. Almost every North American songbird threatened by the destruction of its winter home is also suffering from habitat loss on its breeding grounds. This is true for Sprague's Pipit, McCown's Longspur, and Baird's Sparrow, all birds that winter north of the Rio Grande. It is true for the Swainson's and Worm-eating Warblers that winter in the West Indies and Central America.

It is particularly true for the Cerulean Warbler. The decline of the Cerulean—between 1966 and 1982, the most rapid of any North American warbler—has been blamed equally on loss of the bottomland forest where it breeds and the destruction of the humid evergreen forests on the Andean foothills where it winters.

Bachman's Warbler, never a common bird, may now be extinct. As far as we can tell, the entire population wintered in Cuba, where almost all of the winter habitat was converted to sugar cane early in this century. The loss of the bird, though, may have as much to do with the loss of canebrakes in the bottomlands of the southeastern United States as with the fate of its wintering ground.

If the whole problem were on the wintering grounds, we would expect to see migrant songbirds in decline everywhere. We do not. Birds breeding in large forests such as the ones in Great Smoky Mountains National Park in Tennessee seem relatively safe. The same birds breeding in isolated small woodlots are far less secure. The biggest problem woodlot birds may have is not that their wintering areas are being destroyed, but that the forests where they breed have been cut into such small pieces—a process called *fragmentation*.

Fragmentation has actually benefitted some species, because the more you cut a forest into small patches, the more forest edge you create. The American Robin was once much less common than it is today. John James Audubon saw a Chestnut-sided Warbler only twice in his life. Today, these birds of edge and second growth are common, while the birds that once lived in the depths of the great uninterrupted forest that formerly blanketed much of eastern North America have withdrawn in the face of the European advance. Blue Jays and Red-winged Blackbirds, too, are far commoner today than they were two centuries ago.

Why does fragmentation pose such a threat to the songbirds of the forest interior? Small woodlots may expose birds to too much disturbance, or not provide the range of foods, or places to nest, that birds can find in a larger forest. Though a Wood Thrush may nest in a wooded patch no bigger than two and a half acres (1 ha), some songbirds will not live in woodlots at all unless they are large enough to contain many territories. Male Ovenbirds in small forest patches are less likely to find a mate than males in larger forests. The biggest problems for woodlot birds, though, are the predators and parasites that hunt along all that additional forest edge.

Raccoons, Blue Jays, and Common Grackles hunt along the forest edge, and are much more likely to prey on eggs or young in small woodlots than in larger tracts. Nest predators may take so many young in small forest patches that they make it impossible for the birds trying to breed there to maintain themselves. Eighty percent of open-cup nests in six small woodlots in Illinois were destroyed by predators. Although nesting close to the edge of a forest appears to make no difference for birds in northern Minnesota with open-cup nests, in Pennsylvania, Ovenbirds in a large tract of forest, greater than twenty-five thousand acres (10 000 ha), had ten times the nesting success of the same species in eleven small forest patches.

Brown-headed Cowbirds will not penetrate far into a forest, but they can reach the interior of a small woodlot and parasitize most of the small songbirds that live there. A young cowbird is so much larger and more demanding than its usual hosts that it greatly affects their efforts to feed their own young. In Illinois, 65 percent of the nests of small songbirds in forest patches contained cowbird eggs. Few of the hosts succeeded in raising their own young. A Wood Thrush can raise its own young even with cowbird eggs in its nest, but when a cowbird lays its egg it may toss out some of the thrush's eggs. Even Wood Thrush nests as deep as 1,300 feet (400 m) from the edge of the forest suffered between 80 and 100 percent cowbird parasitism.

The Wood Thrush is still a common bird in eastern North America, but that may not last. It winters almost entirely in the depths of lowland primary forests of Central America, and these forests are fast disappearing. In Pennsylvania, more than 80 percent of the Wood Thrush nests in large forests fledged young, but less than half succeeded in small woodlots. Fifty-six percent of the nests in forest patches of less than two hundred acres (80 ha) were lost to predators, as compared with only 10 percent in a forest greater than twenty-five thousand acres (10 000 ha) in area. Cowbirds made little difference; for some reason, they are not the problem for birds on the eastern seaboard that they are in the Midwest.

It may be that the Wood Thrushes and other songbirds we see in woodlots today would not be there if breeding grounds in the few really large, unfragmented forests of the eastern United States were not still supplying them. David Wilcove did not see a single cowbird in nine weeks of fieldwork in Great Smoky Mountains National Park in Tennessee.

Kirtland's Warbler is an extremely localized species of the jack pine forests in Michigan, whose decline was once blamed entirely on cowbirds. Cowbirds certainly affect it—Kirtland's nests with cowbird eggs produce nearly 40 percent fewer young than normal. In 1957, 55 percent of Kirtland's nests were parasitized by cowbirds. By 1971, this had risen to 69 percent, and the population of singing males had dropped from more than 500 to 201. Over the next twenty years, from 1972 through 1992, the U.S. Fish and Wildlife Service trapped and removed 84,937 cowbirds from Kirtland's Warbler nesting areas. Breeding success increased almost immediately—but warbler numbers stayed about the same.

A victim of forest fragmentation, increased nest predation, and parasitism by growing numbers of Brown-headed Cowbirds, the Wood Thrush, though still common in many places, has become a species carefully watched by North American conservationists.

Cowbirds, it seemed, were not the only problem. Kirtland's Warbler requires stands of jack pine at a specific stage of growth, interspersed with open areas. To make sure that there is enough of this habitat available, you need a fire every now and again. The people trying to save the warbler did not understand this at first and tried to control the fires. In 1980, though, a wildfire swept through nearly ten thousand acres (4000 ha) at Mack Lake, Michigan. The burned-over area started to grow back, and by the late eighties, it had become high-quality warbler habitat. The result was dramatic: the number of singing males rose from 212 in 1989 to 397 in 1992. If Kirtland's Warbler is to thrive, not only does it needs protection from cowbirds—it needs to have enough of the right kind of country.

Forest species get most of the attention, but our grassland birds may be in even worse shape. Grassland birds that became common in the northeastern United States and Canada after the forests were cleared, such as Vesper Sparrows and Eastern Meadowlarks, are now rare again in many areas. Bobolinks, Dickcissels, and Grasshopper, Savannah, and Henslow's Sparrows declined by more than 90 percent in Illinois during the sixties and seventies. Except for the Bobolink and the Dickcissel, most of these birds winter in the United States. Loss and fragmentation of breeding habitat, this time usually caused by intensive farming and urban sprawl, are the likeliest causes of their decline.

For a bird like Henslow's Sparrow any stand of grass will not do. Henslow's needs areas of tall, dense grass that must be at least twenty-five acres (10 ha) in size and have not been disturbed for several years. The sparrows must constantly shift to new areas as their old territories fill with growing trees. Recently, suitable areas, and Henslow's Sparrows, have become harder and harder to find.

What is happening in North America is happening, often to an even greater degree, in the rest of the world. The difference is that here, we have the money and the power to do something about it. In the Tropics, where most of the birds of the world live, even identifying the issues we need to understand in order to prevent a wave of extinctions is far more difficult. Often, the hardest job is making the people with the power to help the situation understand that there is something terribly wrong.

Most tropical songbirds are sedentary creatures restricted to specific habitats. Loss of those habitats will leave them with nowhere else to go. Two thousand eight hundred twenty species of birds live in humid forests in Central and South America. Seventy percent are found nowhere else. Thirty-two percent are found only in one type of humid forest. Two hundred twenty species, including six manakins, nineteen cotingas, and thirty-three tanagers, are found only in montane evergreen forest, which is disappearing everywhere.

The Tropics are full of crisis points for songbird survival—and they are not always where we might expect them to be. Though the rainforests of the Amazon are the richest bird habitat in the world, South America's most endangered birds do not live there. Twenty-six of the thirty-two bird species confined to the distinctive Brazilian Atlantic forest from Rio de Janeiro northward are threatened or endangered, all the others are at risk, and the destruction continues. As little as 3 percent—and certainly no more than 20 percent—of this forest is left.

Grassland birds are disappearing in Brazil, Argentina, Spain, Italy, and India. As the world switches from traditional farming and pasturing techniques to intensified, chemical-dependent modern agriculture, there will be less and less land for these often-ignored species.

Thirty-two of the forty-one species found only in the *cerrado* scrublands of central Brazil, rapidly being devastated by mechanized agriculture, are at risk. The vanishing *campo*, the prairie of central Brazil, has its own endangered birds—the Sharp-tailed Grass-Tyrant and the Campo Miner, for example—but will the world care about birds that most people would dismiss as sparrowy nonentities?

One-quarter of all birds have ranges of less than twenty thousand square miles (50 000 km²). If you plot their ranges on a map, many overlap in special, localized regions called *Endemic Bird Areas*. There are 221 such areas. Together they cover only 5 percent of the world's land surface, but in some countries, such as Indonesia or the Philippines, they include almost every bit

Who will speak up for the Sharp-tailed Grass-Tyrant? How many people have even heard its name? Yet this species is confined to a vanishing habitat, the grasslands of the Brazilian interior, which may be under even more threat than the much more famous rainforests of the Amazon.

of native vegetation that is left. If we lose that 5 percent, we will lose one-quarter of the bird species on earth.

I may appear to be closing this book on too gloomy a note. The world's songbirds, or at least a substantial portion of them, are in trouble, and like the mineshaft Canaries that warned miners of poisonous gases, their decline may be a signal that what we are doing to them will redound on our own heads. I do not mean to say that nothing is being done, or that nothing can be done. I would not have written this book otherwise. Even identifying the problems is a step on the right road. The essay following this chapter will give you some ideas of what you can do to make sure that the worst does not happen. The more you educate yourself about songbirds, appreciate and enjoy them, and turn that knowledge and appreciation into a real effort to help, the greater the chance that songbirds will continue to survive and to thrive. If you and I succeed, we will still be able to watch, and listen, and wonder, as, like Shelley's immortal Skylark,

Higher and still higher
From the earth thou springest
Like a cloud of fire;
The blue deep thou wingest,
And singing still dost soar, and soaring ever singest.

A symbol of failure, a warning for the future, or both? One of the last Dusky Seaside Sparrows sings in a Florida marsh: a sight, and a sound, that we shall never know again.

GETTING INVOLVED

Birders have been at the forefront of the environmental movement for almost a century, and whether you are an active lister, an occasional birder, or a backyard-feeder watcher, you should join them. The birds, and their habitats, need your help.

There is one very simple thing you can do that will save the lives of a great number of songbirds. Cats—even the most harmless-looking house cats—are extraordinarily efficient hunters. They kill tens of millions of birds every year in North America. If you own a cat and you don't want it adding to those statistics, keep it indoors.

While we are on the subject of pets: if you must have pet birds in your house, make sure that you get them from a reputable breeder. Don't become part of the chain that pulls so many birds out of the wild each year. Better still, if you are not planning to make aviculture a serious, intensive pursuit, stick to species of birds that have been bred to be pets for generations. There is nothing wrong with Canaries!

Pets aside, the two best things you can do to help birds are to educate yourself on the issues and to get involved with organizations that are working to save them or their habitats. Your contribution can be as limited as mailing a check. There are, though, programs that let—indeed, are anxious for—you to do more.

The Fatal Lights Awareness Program (FLAP), for example, is a volunteer effort that began in Toronto in 1993. FLAP now operates in Calgary, Edmonton, and New York City, and is spreading to other cities in Canada and the United States. It has two objectives: to rescue night-migrating birds that have become trapped among brightly lit city skyscrapers, and to convince the corporations that own these structures to dim their lights during peak migration times. If you are the sort of birder who doesn't mind getting up before dawn, not to head out to the woods, but to go downtown (for a good cause), FLAP may be for you. To find out whether a FLAP program is operating in your city, you can write FLAP at 1 Guelph Road, Erin, Ontario, Canada N0B 1T0. If there isn't, you might want to start one yourself.

One of Cornell University's Citizen Science projects is specifically designed to track the declines of North American forest birds. It is called Birds in Forested Landscapes, or BFL for short. As a BFL participant, you will visit selected forest sites at least twice each breeding season, search for the birds that the project is interested in—forest thrushes, at the moment—and report your findings to the Cornell Laboratory of Ornithology, 159 Sapsucker Woods Road, Ithaca, New York, U.S.A. 14850. Your findings may help develop recommendations for stopping the loss of our songbirds in small forest patches.

You can help our migrant songbirds with your morning coffee. Traditionally, coffee is grown in the shade of other trees. A shade coffee plantation can be valuable habitat for birds, including North American migrants. However, over the past twenty years or so shade-grown coffee has been replaced in many areas by so-called sun coffee. Sun coffee is grown in the open, and—with plenty of fertilizer and intensive labor—does produce a higher yield. More coffee, though, does not mean a higher yield of birds. The replacement of shade coffee with sun coffee destroys a great deal of bird habitat. Baltimore Orioles, for example, seem to prefer shade-grown coffee plantations in winter. Since about 1980, when the change to sun coffee began in earnest, the Baltimore Oriole has declined over much of North America. In Jamaica, more than twice as many migrant species live in shade coffee plantations as in sun coffee stands. In Central America, almost none of the forest birds that thrive in shaded plantations live in stands of sun coffee. If you choose shade-grown coffee, or ask the stores where you buy coffee to carry it, you are choosing a better habitat for birds. Get the facts from the Smithsonian Migratory Bird Center, National Zoological Park, Washington, D.C., U.S.A. 20008, or from their Web site at http://www.si.edu/natzoo/zooview/smbc/smbchome.htm.

The problems songbirds—and the rest of we living things—face are growing in both number and complexity. The more you become involved with birds, the more you are bound to come face to face with the threats to their survival—and with the solutions to them. I hope, if our forests are not to fall silent after tens of millions of years of song, that the solutions will prevail. They will have a better chance of doing so if you and I become a part of them. It's up to us.

AMERICAN BIRDING ASSOCIATION CODE

PRINCIPLES OF BIRDING ETHICS

Everyone who enjoys birds and birding must always respect wildlife, its environment, and the rights of others.

In any conflict of interest between birds and birders, the welfare of the birds and their environment comes first.

CODE OF BIRDING ETHICS

1. Promote the welfare of birds and their environment.

1(a) Support the protection of important bird habitat.

1(b) To avoid stressing birds or exposing them to danger, exercise restraint and caution during observation, photography, sound recording, or filming.

- Limit the use of recordings and other methods of attracting birds, and never use such methods in heavily birded areas, or for attracting any species that is Threatened, Endangered, or of Special Concern, or is a rare breeder in your local area.

- Keep well back from nests and nesting colonies, roosts, display areas, and important feeding sites. In such sensitive areas, if there is a need for extended observation, photography, filming, or recording, try to use a blind or hide, and take advantage of natural cover.

- Use artificial light sparingly for filming or photography, especially for close-ups.

1(c) Before advertising the presence of a rare bird, evaluate the potential for disturbance to the bird, its surroundings, and other people in the area, and proceed only if access can be controlled, disturbance minimized, and permission has been obtained from private land-owners.

The sites of rare nesting birds should be divulged only to the proper conservation authorities.

1(d) Stay on roads, trails, and paths where they exist; otherwise keep habitat disturbance to a minimum.

2. Respect the law, and the rights of others.

2(a) Do not enter private property without the owner's explicit permission.

2(b) Follow all laws, rules, and regulations governing the use of roads and public areas, both at home and abroad.

2(c) Practice common courtesy in contacts with other people. Your exemplary behavior will generate goodwill with birders and non-birders alike.

3. Ensure that feeders, nest structures, and other artificial bird environments are safe.

3(a) Keep dispensers, water, and food clean and free of decay or disease. It is important to feed birds continually during harsh weather.

3(b) Maintain and clean nest structures regularly.

3(c) If you are attracting birds to an area, ensure the birds are not exposed to predation from cats and other domestic animals, or dangers posed by artificial hazards.

4. Group birding, whether organized or impromptu, requires special care.

Each individual in the group, in addition to the obligations spelled out in Items #1 and #2, has responsibilities as a Group Member.

4(a) Respect the interests, rights, and skills of fellow birders, as well as people participating in other legitimate outdoor activities. Freely share your knowledge and experience, except where code 1(c) applies. Be especially helpful to beginning birders.

4(b) If you witness unethical birding behavior, assess the situation and intervene if you think it prudent. When interceding, inform the person(s) of the inappropriate action and attempt, within reason, to have it stopped. If the behavior continues, document it and notify appropriate individuals or organizations.

Group Leader Responsibilities (for amateur and professional trips and tours).

4(d) Be an exemplary ethical role model for the group. Teach through word and example.

4(e) Keep groups to a size that limits impact on the environment and does not interfere with others using the same area.

4(f) Ensure everyone in the group knows of and practices this code.

4(g) Learn and inform the group of any special circumstances applicable to the areas being visited (e.g., no tape recorders allowed).

4(h) Acknowledge that professional tour companies bear a special responsibility to place the welfare of birds and the benefits of public knowledge ahead of the company's commercial interests. Ideally, leaders should keep track of tour sightings, document unusual occurrences, and submit records to appropriate organizations.

PLEASE FOLLOW THIS CODE, AND DISTRIBUTE AND TEACH IT TO OTHERS.

SONGBIRD RESOURCES

I have space here to list only a few of the many resources available to birders and bird students in North America. They should be enough to get you started. For many more, see Sheila Buff's *The Birder's Sourcebook: A Compendium of Essential Birding Information*, published in 1994 by Lyons and Burford.

If I mention a commercial service in this section, that mention is not to be taken as an endorsement, or in any way to imply that the service is better than others I may have overlooked.

National Organizations
American Birding Association
P.O. Box 6599
Colorado Springs, CO 80934
1-800-850-2473

Canadian Nature Federation
453 Sussex Drive
Ottawa, ON K1N 6Z4
1-613-238-6154

Cornell Laboratory of Ornithology
159 Sapsucker Woods Road
Ithaca, NY 14850
1-607-254- 2000

National Audubon Society
700 Broadway
New York, NY 10003
1-212-979-3000

Birding Magazines
Of the organizations listed above, the American Birding Association publishes *Birding* and a newsletter, *Winging It*; the Canadian Nature Federation publishes *Nature Canada*; the Cornell Laboratory of Ornithology publishes *Living Bird Quarterly*; and the National

Audubon Society publishes *Audubon and American Birds*. Other nontechnical periodicals on birds include:

Birder's World
44 East Eighth Street, Suite 410
Holland, MI 49423
1-616-396-5618

Birds of the Wild
P.O. Box 73
Markham, ON L3P 3J5
1-905-294-0303

BirdWatcher's Digest
P.O. Box 110
Marietta, OH 45750
1-800-421-9764

WildBird Magazine
P.O. Box 57900
Los Angeles, CA 90057
1-213-385-5222

Field Guides

These are the most widely used field guides in North America:

National Geographic Society. *Field Guide to the Birds of North America*. 2d ed. 1987 (1992).

Peterson, Roger Tory. *A Field Guide to the Birds East of the Rockies*. 4th ed. Boston: Houghton Mifflin, 1980.

Peterson, Roger Tory. *A Field Guide to Western Birds*. 3d ed. Boston: Houghton Mifflin, 1990.

Robbins, Chandler S., Bertel Bruun, and Herbert S. Zim. *Birds of North America: A Guide to Field Identification*. rev. and expand. ed. New York: Golden Press, 1983.

Attracting Birds

These books (or others like them) should give you some good ideas:

Dennis, J. V., and M. McKinley. *How to Attract Birds*. San Ramon, CA: Ortho Books, 1994.

Kress, Stephen W. *The Bird Garden: A Comprehensive Guide to Attracting Birds to Your Backyard throughout the Year*. New York: National Audubon Society/Dorling Kindersley, 1995.

Soper, Tony. *The Bird Table Book*. 6th ed. Newton Abbot, Devon: David and Charles, 1992.

Stokes, Donald, and Lillian Stokes. *The Bluebird Book*. Boston: Little, Brown and Co., 1991.

Terres, John K. *Songbirds in Your Garden*. rev. and expand. ed. Chapel Hill: Algonquin Books, 1994.

Waldon, Bob. *A Guide to Feeding Winter Birds in British Columbia*. Vancouver: Whitecap Books, 1992.

Helping Birds

In addition to the ideas mentioned in the main text, you can find other ways to help birds survive in:

Greenberg, Russell, and Jamie Reaser. *Bring Back the Birds: What You Can Do to Save Threatened Species*. Mechanicsburg, PA: Stackpole Books, 1995.

Finding Birds

There are a number of bird-finding guides to different parts of North America, but this one covers the whole continent:

Cooper, Jerry A. *Birdfinder: A Birder's Guide to Planning North American Trips*. Colorado Springs: American Birding Association, 1995.

Cyber-Birding

Songbird sites on the World Wide Web range from *The Electronic Nuthatch* at

http://alt-www.uia.ac.be/u/matthys/nuthatch.html

to *Songbird Brain Circuitry* at

http://www.williams.edu:803/Biology/ZFinch/circuits.html

The most complete list of bird-related links I know is the *Bird Links to the World* page at

http://www.ntic.qc.ca/~nellus/links.html,

operated by Denis LePage from Quebec. It will lead you to hundreds of sites. You can also check out *Birding on the Web* at

http://wwwstat.wharton.upenn.edu/~siler/birding.html

and the *Birder Home Page* at

http://www.birder.com/

—perhaps the best place for a beginner to start.

You can order almost any book on birds (or any other natural history topic) online from the *Natural History Book Service* at

http://www.nhbs.co.uk/nhbsmain.html

or from *Buteo Books* at

http://www.datacity.com/buteo/

For a more interactive experience, you can check out usenet newsgroups such as rec.birds, uk.rec.birdwatching, and others—or, better still, join an Internet mailing list such as BirdChat. To join BirdChat, send a message to

listserv@listserv.arizona.edu

with the text "subscribe birdchat [your name]." I'll see you there!

FURTHER READING

There are a great many books about songbirds. The following list includes only some of the more recent ones I consulted while writing this book. Those marked with an asterisk (*) are quite technical, intended primarily for professional ornithologists.

General

Alcock, John. *The Kookaburra's Song: Exploring Animal Behavior in Australia*. Tucson: University of Arizona Press, 1988.

Campbell, Bruce, and Elizabeth Lack, eds. *A Dictionary of Birds*. London: T. and A. D. Poyser, 1985.

Ehrlich, P. R., D. S. Dobkin, and D. Wheye. *The Birder's Handbook*. New York: Simon and Schuster, 1988.

Gill, Frank. *Ornithology*. 2d ed. New York: W. H. Freeman and Co., 1994.

Hilty, Steven. *Birds of Tropical America: A Watcher's Introduction to Behavior, Breeding and Diversity*. Shelburne, VT: Chapters, 1994.

Hudson, W. H. *The Bird Biographies of W. H. Hudson*. Selected from *Birds of La Plata*. Santa Barbara: Capra Press, 1988.

Kaufman, Kenn. *Lives of North American Birds*. Boston: Houghton Mifflin, 1996.

Skutch, Alexander F. *The Minds of Birds*. College Station: Texas A & M University Press, 1996.

Terres, John K. *The Audubon Society Encyclopedia of North American Birds*. New York: Knopf, 1980 (1995).

Conservation

Berger, Andrew J. *Hawaiian Birdlife*. 2d ed. Honolulu: University of Hawaii Press, 1981.

Collar, N. J., M. J. Crosby, and A. J. Stattersfield. *Birds to Watch 2: The World List of Threatened Birds*. Cambridge: BirdLife International, 1994.

Jaffe, Mark. *And No Birds Sing: The Story of an Ecological Disaster in a Tropical Paradise (Guam)*. New York: Simon and Schuster, 1994.

*Moors, P. J., ed. *Conservation of Island Birds. Case Studies for the Management of Threatened Island Species*. ICBP Technical Publication No. 3. Cambridge: BirdLife International, 1985.

*Stolz, Douglas F., J. W. Fitzpatrick, T. A. Parker III, and D. K. Moskovits. *Neotropical Birds: Ecology and Conservation*. Chicago and London: University of Chicago Press, 1996.

Terborgh, John. *Where Have All the Birds Gone?: Essays on the Biology and Conservation of Birds That Migrate to the American Tropics*. Princeton: Princeton University Press, 1989.

Walters, Mark Jerome. *A Shadow and a Song: The Extinction of the Dusky Seaside Sparrow.* Post Mills, VT: Chelsea Green Publishing Co., 1992.

Evolution

Feduccia, Alan. *The Origin and Evolution of Birds.* New Haven: Yale University Press, 1996.

Jobling, James A. *A Dictionary of Scientific Bird Names.* Oxford: Oxford University Press, 1991.

Mock, Douglas W., ed. *Behavior and Evolution of Birds: Readings from Scientific American Magazine.* New York: W. H. Freeman and Co., 1991.

Sibley, Charles G., and Burt L. Monroe Jr. *Distribution and Taxonomy of Birds of the World.* New Haven: Yale University Press, 1991 (supplement published 1993).

Life History

*Black, Jeffrey M., ed. *Partnerships in Birds: The Study of Monogamy.* Oxford: Oxford University Press, 1996.

*Carey, Cynthia, ed. *Avian Energetics and Nutritional Ecology.* New York: Chapman and Hall, 1996.

Johnsgard, Paul A. *Arena Birds: Sexual Selection and Behavior.* Washington, D.C.: Smithsonian Institution Press, 1994.

Skutch, Alexander F. *Birds Asleep.* Austin: University of Texas Press, 1989.

Migration

*Alerstam, Thomas. *Bird Migration.* Cambridge: Cambridge University Press, 1990.

Elphick, Jonathan, ed. *The Atlas of Bird Migration.* New York: Random House, 1995.

*Rappole, John. *The Ecology of Migrant Birds: A Neotropical Perspective.* Washington, D.C.: Smithsonian Institution Press, 1995.

Song

Catchpole, C. K., and P. J. B. Slater. *Bird Song: Biological Themes and Variations.* Cambridge: Cambridge University Press, 1995.

Specific Songbirds

Bruggers, Richard L., and Clive C. H. Elliott, eds. Quelea quelea: *Africa's Bird Pest.* Oxford: Oxford University Press, 1989.

Davies, N. B. *Dunnock Behavior and Social Evolution.* Oxford: Oxford University Press, 1992.

Grant, Peter R. *Ecology and Evolution of Darwin's Finches.* Princeton: Princeton University Press, 1986.

Kilham, Lawrence. *The American Crow and the Common Raven.* College Station: Texas A & M University Press, 1989.

Lambert, Frank, and M. Woodcock. *Pittas, Broadbills and Asities.* East Sussex: Pica Press, 1996.

Lundberg, Arne, and Rauno V. Alatalo. *The Pied Flycatcher.* London: T. and A. D. Poyser, 1992.

Madge, Steve, and Hilary Burn. *Crows and Jays: A Guide to the Crows, Jays and Magpies of the World.* Boston: Houghton Mifflin, 1994.

Marzluff, John M., and Russel P. Balda. *The Pinyon Jay: Behavioral Ecology of a Colonial and Cooperative Corvid.* London: T. and A. D. Poyser, 1992.

*Møller, Anders P. *Sexual Selection and the Barn Swallow.* Oxford: Oxford University Press, 1994.

Morse, Douglass H. *American Warblers: An Ecological and Behavioral Perspective.* Cambridge, MA: Harvard University Press, 1989.

Orians, Gordon H. *Blackbirds of the Americas.* Seattle: University of Washington Press, 1985.

Reilly, Pauline. *The Lyrebird. A Natural History.* Kensington, NSW: New South Wales University Press, 1988.

Restall, Robin. *Munias and Mannikins.* East Sussex: Pica Press, 1996.

Rising, James D. *A Guide to the Identification and Natural History of the Sparrows of the United States and Canada.* San Diego: Academic Press, 1996.

*Searcy, William A., and Ken Yasukawa. *Polygyny and Sexual Selection in Red-Winged Blackbirds.* Princeton: Princeton University Press, 1995.

Skutch, Alexander F. *Antbirds and Ovenbirds: Their Lives and Homes.* Austin: University of Texas Press, 1996.

Skutch, Alexander F. *Orioles, Blackbirds and Their Kin: A Natural History.* Tucson: University of Arizona Press, 1996.

Smith, Susan M. *The Black-Capped Chickadee: Behavioral Ecology and Natural History.* Ithaca and London: Comstock Publishing Associates, 1991.

Snow, David W. *The Cotingas: Bellbirds, Umbrellabirds and Other Species.* Ithaca: Cornell University Press, 1982.

Summers-Smith, J. Denis. *The Tree Sparrow.* Published by the author, 1995.

Tyler, Stephanie, and Stephen Ormerod. *The Dippers.* London: T. and A. D. Poyser, 1994.

SPECIES MENTIONED IN THIS BOOK

The following list gives the English and scientific names for all bird species mentioned in this book. All are songbirds, except for those marked with an asterisk (*). The third column indicates, in code, the major zoogeographic region(s) of the world where the bird breeds. These are: AF—Afrotropical Region (Africa south of the Sahara, including Madagascar and the Seychelles); AU—Australasian Region (Australia; New Guinea; Indonesia, from Lombok and Sulawesi eastward; and the Pacific islands, including Hawaii); NA—Nearctic Region (North America south to the Isthmus of Tehuantepec, Mexico, including Greenland); NT—Neotropical Region (Central and South America, including the West Indies, Galápagos, Falklands, South Georgia, and the Tristan group); OR—Oriental Region (Southeast Asia, including the Philippines and Indonesia east to Bali and Borneo); PA—Palaearctic Region (Europe; temperate Asia, including Japan; and North Africa).

Accentor, Alpine	*Prunella collaris*	PA
Accentor, Japanese	*Prunella rubida*	PA
Akekee	*Loxops caeruleirostris*	AU
Akepa	*Loxops coccineus*	AU
Akialoa	*Hemignathus obscurus*	AU
Akiapolaau	*Hemignathus wilsoni*	AU
Antbird, Bicolored	*Gymnopithys bicolor*	NT
Antbird, Ocellated	*Phaenostictus mcleannani*	NT
Antbird, Spotted	*Hylophylax naevioides*	NT
Antbird, White-plumed	*Pithys albifrons*	NT
Antshrike, Barred	*Thamnophilus doliatus*	NT
Antshrike, Bluish-slate	*Thamnomanes schistogynus*	NT
Antshrike, Dusky-throated (Saturnine)	*Thamnomanes ardesiacus*	NT
Antthrush, Black-faced	*Formicarius analis*	NT
Astrapia, Ribbon-tailed	*Astrapia mayeri*	AU
Avadavat, Red	*Amandava amandava*	OR
Babbler, Gray-crowned	*Pomatostomus temporalis*	AU
Babbler, Jungle	*Turdoides striatus*	OR
Babbler, Southern Pied	*Turdoides bicolor*	AF
Bananaquit	*Coereba flaveola*	NT
Bare-Eye, Black-spotted	*Phlegopsis nigromaculata*	NT
Bellbird, Bare-throated	*Procnias nudicollis*	NT
Bellbird, New Zealand	*Anthornis melanura*	AU
Bellbird, Three-wattled	*Procnias tricarunculata*	NT
Bird-of-Paradise, Blue	*Paradisaea rudolphi*	AU
Bird-of-Paradise, King	*Cicinnurus regius*	AU
Bird-of-Paradise, King of Saxony	*Pteridophora alberti*	AU
Bird-of-Paradise, Lesser	*Paradisaea minor*	AU
Bird-of-Paradise, Magnificent	*Cicinnurus magnificus*	AU
Bird-of-Paradise, Raggiana	*Paradisaea raggiana*	AU
Bird-of-Paradise, Red	*Paradisaea rubra*	AU
Bird-of-Paradise, Twelve-wired	*Seleucidis melanoleuca*	AU
Bird-of-Paradise, Wilson's	*Cicinnurus respublica*	AU
Blackbird, European	*Turdus merula*	PA
Blackbird, Jamaican	*Nesopsar nigerrimus*	NT
Blackbird, Red-winged	*Agelaius phoeniceus*	NA
Blackbird, Saffron-cowled	*Agelaius flavus*	NT
Blackbird, Scarlet-headed	*Amblyramphus holosericeus*	NT
Blackbird, Yellow-headed	*Xanthocephalus xanthocephalus*	NA
Blackbird, Yellow-hooded	*Agelaius icterocephalus*	NT
Blackbird, Yellow-shouldered	*Agelaius xanthomus*	NT
Bluebird, Eastern	*Sialia sialis*	NA
Bluethroat	*Luscinia svecica*	PA
Bobolink	*Dolichonyx oryzivorus*	NA
Boobies, Masked*	*Sula dactylatra*	all regions
Boubou, Slate-colored	*Laniarius funebris*	AF
Bowerbird, Flame	*Sericulus aureus*	AU
Bowerbird, Golden	*Prionodura newtoniana*	AU
Bowerbird, Golden-crested	*Archboldia sanfordi*	AU
Bowerbird, Great	*Chlamydera nuchalis*	AU
Bowerbird, MacGregor's	*Amblyornis macgregoriae*	AU
Bowerbird, Satin	*Ptilonorhynchus violaceus*	AU
Bowerbird, Spotted	*Chlamydera maculata*	AU
Bowerbird, Streaked	*Amblyornis subalaris*	AU
Bowerbird, Tooth-billed	*Ailuroedus dentirostris*	AU
Bowerbird, Vogelkop	*Amblyornis inornatus*	AU
Bowerbird, Yellow-breasted	*Chlamydera lauterbachi*	AU
Bristlehead, Bornean	*Pityriasis gymnocephala*	OR
Broadbill, African	*Smithornis capensis*	AF
Broadbill, Black-and-red	*Cymbirhynchus macrorhynchos*	OR
Broadbill, Dusky	*Corydon sumatranus*	OR
Broadbill, Green	*Calyptomena viridis*	OR
Buffalo-Weaver, White-headed	*Dinemellia dinemelli*	AF
Bulbul, Red-whiskered	*Pycnonotus jocosus*	OR
Bulbul, Straw-headed	*Pycnonotus zeylanicus*	OR
Bulbul, Yellow-bellied	*Chlorocichla flaviventris*	AF
Bullfinch	*Pyrrhula pyrrhula*	PA
Bullfinch, Puerto Rican	*Loxigilla portoricensis*	NT
Bunting, Corn	*Miliaria calandra*	PA
Bunting, Indigo	*Passerina cyanea*	NA
Bunting, McKay's	*Plectrophenax hyperboreus*	NA
Bunting, Reed	*Emberiza schoeniclus*	PA
Bunting, Snow	*Plectrophenax nivalis*	NA, PA
Bush-Tanager, Sooty-capped	*Chlorospingus pileatus*	NT
Bushbird, Recurve-billed	*Clytoctantes alixii*	NT
Bushtit	*Psaltriparus minimus*	NA
Butcherbird, Pied	*Cracticus nigrogularis*	AU
Cacholote, Brown	*Pseudoseisura lophotes*	NT
Cacholote, White-throated	*Pseudoseisura gutturalis*	NT
Cacique, Yellow-rumped	*Cacicus cela*	NT
Cactus-Finch, Large	*Geospiza conirostris*	NT
Calyptura, Kinglet	*Calyptura cristata*	NT
Canary	*Serinus canaria*	PA
Canastero, Hudson's	*Asthenes hudsoni*	NT
Caracara, Chimango*	*Milvago chimango*	NT
Cardinal, Northern	*Cardinalis cardinalis*	NA
Cardinal, Red-crested	*Paroaria coronata*	NT
Cardinal, Yellow	*Gubernatrix cristata*	NT
Catbird, Gray	*Dumetella carolinensis*	NA
Chaffinch	*Fringilla coelebs*	PA
Chaffinch, Blue	*Fringilla teydea*	PA
Chat, Yellow-breasted	*Icteria virens*	NA
Chickadee, Black-capped	*Parus atricapillus*	NA
Chickadee, Chestnut-backed	*Parus rufescens*	NA
Chickadee, Gray-headed (see Tit, Siberian)		
Chiffchaff	*Phylloscopus collybita*	PA
Chowchilla	*Orthonyx spaldingii*	AU
Cinclodes, Blackish	*Cinclodes antarcticus*	NT

Cinclodes, Long-tailed	*Cinclodes pabsti*	NT	Finch, Trumpeter	*Rhodopechys githaginea*	PA
Cinclodes, Seaside	*Cinclodes nigrofumosus*	NT	Finch, Warbler	*Certhidea olivacea*	NT
Cock-of-the-Rock, Andean	*Rupicola peruviana*	NT	Finch, Woodpecker	*Camarhynchus pallidus*	NT
Cock-of-the-Rock, Guianan	*Rupicola rupicola*	NT	Finch, Zebra	*Taeniopygia guttata*	AU
Cotinga, Pompadour	*Xipholena punicea*	NT	Finch-Lark, Black-eared	*Eremopterix australis*	AF
Cowbird, Bay-winged	*Molothrus badius*	NT	Firefinch, Jameson's	*Lagonosticta rhodopareia*	AF
Cowbird, Brown-headed	*Molothrus ater*	NA	Firefinch, Red-billed	*Lagonosticta senegala*	AF
Cowbird, Giant	*Scaphidura oryzivora*	NT	Firetail, Beautiful	*Stagonopleura bella*	AU
Cowbird, Screaming	*Molothrus rufoaxillaris*	NT	Firetail, Diamond	*Stagonopleura guttata*	AU
Cowbird, Shiny	*Molothrus bonariensis*	NT	Firetail, Red-browed	*Neochmia temporalis*	AU
Creeper, Brown	*Certhia americana*	NA	Firewood-Gatherer	*Anumbius annumbi*	NT
Crossbill, Parrot	*Loxia pytyopsittacus*	PA	Flicker, Northern*	*Colaptes auratus*	NA
Crossbill, Red	*Loxia curvirostra*	NA, PA	Flowerpecker, Cebu	*Dicaeum quadricolor*	OR
Crossbill, Scottish	*Loxia scotica*	PA	Flower-piercer, Masked	*Diglossopis cyanea*	NT
Crossbill, White-winged	*Loxia leucoptera*	NA, PA	Flycatcher, Collared	*Ficedula albicollis*	PA
Crow, American	*Corvus brachyrhynchos*	NA	Flycatcher, Dohrn's	*Horizorhinus dohrni*	AF
Crow, Hawaiian	*Corvus hawaiiensis*	AU	Flycatcher, Great Crested	*Myiarchus crinitus*	NA
Crow, New Caledonian	*Corvus moneduloides*	AU	Flycatcher, Guam	*Myiagra freycineti*	AU
Crow, Northwestern	*Corvus caurinus*	NA	Flycatcher, Least	*Empidonax minimus*	NA
Cuckoo, Common*	*Cuculus canorus*	PA	Flycatcher, Olive-sided	*Contopus borealis*	NA
Cuckooshrike, New Guinea Black	*Coracina melas*	AU	Flycatcher, Pied	*Ficedula hypoleuca*	PA
Currawong, Pied	*Strepera graculina*	AU	Flycatcher, Piratic	*Legatus leucophaius*	NT
Dickcissel	*Spiza americana*	NA	Flycatcher, Royal	*Onychorhynchus coronatus*	NT
Dipper, American	*Cinclus mexicanus*	NA	Flycatcher, Satin	*Myiagra cyanoleuca*	AU
Dipper, Brown	*Cinclus pallasii*	PA	Flycatcher, Scissor-tailed	*Tyrannus forficatus*	NT
Dipper, White-throated	*Cinclus cinclus*	PA	Flycatcher, Spotted	*Muscicapa striata*	PA
Diuca-Finch, Common	*Diuca diuca*	NT	Flycatcher, Sulfur-rumped	*Myiobius barbatus*	NT
Drongo, Fork-tailed	*Dicrurus adsimilis*	AF	Flycatcher, Variegated	*Empidonomus varius*	NT
Dunnock	*Prunella modularis*	PA	Flycatcher, Vermilion	*Pyrocephalus rubinus*	NA, NT
Egret, Great*	*Casmerodius albus*	all regions	Flycatcher, Willow	*Empidonax traillii*	NA
Elaenia, White-crested	*Elaenia albiceps*	NT	Forest-Falcon, Slaty-backed*	*Micrastur mirandollei*	NA
Elaenia, Yellow-bellied	*Elaenia flavogaster*	NT	Friarbird, Noisy	*Philemon corniculatus*	AU
Elepaio	*Chasiempis sandwichensis*	AU	Gibberbird	*Ashbyia lovensis*	AU
Emu*	*Dromaius novaehollandiae*	AU	Gnatcatcher, Black-tailed	*Polioptila melanura*	NA
Emu-Wren, Mallee	*Stipiturus mallee*	AU	Gnatcatcher, Blue-gray	*Polioptila caerulea*	NA
Euphonia, Thick-billed	*Euphonia laniirostris*	NT	Gnatcatcher, California	*Polioptila californica*	NA
Euphonia, Yellow-throated	*Euphonia hirundinacea*	NT	Goldcrest	*Regulus regulus*	PA
Fairy-Wren, Splendid	*Malurus splendens*	AU	Goldfinch, American	*Carduelis tristis*	NA
Fairy-Wren, Superb [Blue Wren]	*Malurus cyaneus*	AU	Gonolek, Black-headed	*Laniarius erythrogaster*	AF
Fairy-Wren, White-winged	*Malurus leucopterus*	AU	Goshawk, Gabar*	*Micronisus gabar*	AF
Falcon, Eleonora's*	*Falco eleonorae*	PA	Grackle, Common	*Quiscalus quiscula*	NA
Falcon, Sooty*	*Falco concolor*	PA	Grass-Tyrant, Sharp-tailed	*Culicivora caudacuta*	NT
Fantail, Rufous	*Rhipidura rufifrons*	AU	Greenbul, Bearded	*Criniger barbatus*	AF
Fieldfare	*Turdus pilaris*	PA, NA	Greenbul, Yellow-whiskered	*Andropadus latirostris*	AF
Finch, Gouldian	*Chloebia gouldiae*	AU	Greenlet, Scrub	*Hylophilus flavipes*	NT
Finch, House	*Carpodacus mexicanus*	NA	Greenlet, Tawny-crowned	*Hylophilus ochraceiceps*	NT
Finch, Laysan	*Telespiza cantans*	AU	Grenadier, Purple	*Uraeginthus ianthinogaster*	AF
Finch, Saffron	*Sicalis flaveola*	NT	Grosbeak, Bonin [Islands]	*Chaunoproctus ferreorostris*	PA
Finch, Scaly-feathered	*Sporopipes squamifrons*	AF	Grosbeak, Evening	*Hesperiphona vespertina*	NA

Grosbeak, Kona	*Chloridops kona*	AU
Grosbeak, Pine	*Pinicola enucleator*	NA, PA
Grosbeak, Rose-breasted	*Pheucticus ludovicianus*	NA
Grosbeak, São Tomé	*Neospiza concolor*	AF
Ground-Finch, Large	*Geospiza magnirostris*	NT
Ground-Finch, Medium	*Geospiza fortis*	NT
Ground-Finch, Sharp-beaked	*Geospiza difficilis*	NT
Ground-Finch, Small	*Geospiza fuliginosa*	NT
Hawfinch	*Coccothraustes coccothraustes*	PA
Hawk-Eagle, Crowned*	*Stephanoaetus coronatus*	AF
Hoatzin*	*Opisthocomus hoazin*	NT
Honeyeater, Helmeted	*Lichenostomus melanops cassidix*	AU
Honeyeater, New Holland	*Phylidonyris novaehollandiae*	AU
Honeyeater, White-eared	*Lichenostomus leucotis*	AU
Honeyeater, Yellow-faced	*Lichenostomus chrysops*	AU
Honeyeater, Smoky	*Melipotes fumigatus*	AU
Hornero, Rufous	*Furnarius rufus*	NT
Huia	*Heteralocha acutirostris*	AU
Hummingbird, Giant*	*Patagona gigas*	NT
Ibis, White*	*Guara alba*	NA
Ifrit, Blue-capped	*Ifrita kowaldi*	AU
Iiwi	*Vestiaria coccinea*	AU
Indigobird, Village	*Vidua chalybeata*	AF
Jay, Blue	*Cyanocitta cristata*	NA
Jay, Eurasian	*Garrulus glandarius*	PA
Jay, Florida Scrub	*Aphelocoma coerulescens*	NA
Jay, Gray	*Perisoreus canadensis*	NA
Jay, Mexican	*Aphelocoma ultramarina*	NA
Jay, Pinyon	*Gymnorhinus cyanocephalus*	NA
Jay, Steller's	*Cyanocitta stelleri*	NA
Junco, Yellow-eyed	*Junco phaeonotus*	NA
Kingbird, Eastern	*Tyrannus tyrannus*	NA
Kinglet, Golden-crowned	*Regulus satrapa*	NA
Kinglet, Ruby-crowned	*Regulus calendula*	NA
Kioea	*Chaetoptila angustipluma*	AU
Kiskadee, Greater	*Pitangus sulphuratus*	NA, NT
Kokako	*Callaeas cinerea*	AU
Kookaburra, Laughing*	*Dacelo novaeguineae*	AU
Lark, Desert	*Ammomanes deserti*	PA
Lark, Red	*Certhilauda burra*	AF
Lark, Spike-heeled	*Chersomanes albofasciata*	AF
Longclaw, Yellow-throated	*Macronyx croceus*	AF
Longspur, Lapland	*Calcarius lapponicus*	NA, PA
Longspur, McCown's	*Calcarius mccownii*	NA
Longspur, Smith's	*Calcarius pictus*	NA
Lyrebird, Albert's	*Menura alberti*	AU
Lyrebird, Superb	*Menura novaehollandiae*	AU
Magpie, Australian	*Gymnorhina tibicen*	AU
Magpie, Black-billed	*Pica pica*	NA, PA
Magpie-Robin, Seychelles	*Copsychus sechellarum*	AF
Malimbe, Black-throated	*Malimbus cassini*	AF
Malimbe, Red-bellied	*Malimbus erythrogaster*	AF
Mamo	*Drepanis pacifica*	AU
Manakin, Band-tailed	*Pipra fasciicauda*	NT
Manakin, Club-winged	*Machaeropterus deliciosus*	NT
Manakin, Crimson-hooded	*Pipra aureola*	NT
Manakin, Golden-collared	*Manacus vitellinus*	NT
Manakin, Long-tailed	*Chiroxiphia linearis*	NT
Manakin, Red-capped	*Pipra mentalis*	NT
Manakin, White-bearded	*Manacus manacus*	NT
Manakin, White-ruffed	*Corapipo altera*	NT
Manakin, Wire-tailed	*Pipra filicauda*	NT
Manucode, Trumpet	*Manucodia keraudrenii*	AU
Martin, African River	*Pseudochelidon eurystomina*	AF
Martin, Brown-chested	*Phaeoprogne tapera*	NT
Martin, Purple	*Progne subis*	NA
Martin, Sand (Bank Swallow)	*Riparia riparia*	NA, PA
Meadowlark, Eastern	*Sturnella magna*	NA
Meadowlark, Pampas	*Sturnella militaris*	NT
Meadowlark, Western	*Sturnella neglecta*	NA
Millerbird	*Acrocephalus familiaris*	AU
Miner, Bell	*Manorina melanophrys*	AU
Miner, Campo	*Geobates poecilopterus*	NT
Mistletoebird	*Dicaeum hirundinaceum*	AU
Mockingbird, Northern	*Mimus polyglottos*	NA
Mockingbird, White-banded	*Mimus triurus*	NT
Monarch, Black-faced	*Monarcha melanopsis*	AU
Monarch, Pied	*Arses kaupi*	AU
Monjita, Black-and-white	*Heteroxolmis dominicana*	NT
Myna, Bali	*Leucopsar rothschildi*	OR
Myna, Crested	*Acridotheres cristatellus*	OR
Myna, Finch-billed	*Scissirostrum dubium*	AU
Myna, Hill	*Gracula religiosa*	OR
Myzomela, Ebony	*Myzomela pammelaena*	AU
Myzomela, Scarlet-bibbed	*Myzomela sclateri*	AU
Negrito, Austral	*Lessonia rufa*	NT
Nightingale	*Luscinia megarhynchos*	PA
Nutcracker, Clark's	*Nucifraga columbiana*	NA
Nutcracker, Eurasian	*Nucifraga caryocatactes*	PA
Nuthatch, European	*Sitta europaea*	PA
Nuthatch, Pygmy	*Sitta pygmaea*	NA
Nuthatch, White-breasted	*Sitta carolinensis*	NA
Omao	*Myadestes obscurus*	AU
Oo, Bishop's	*Moho bishopi*	AU
Oo, Hawaii	*Moho nobilis*	AU
Oo, Kauai	*Moho braccatus*	AU
Oo, Oahu	*Moho apicalis*	AU
Orangequit	*Euneornis campestris*	NT

Oriole, Baltimore	*Icterus galbula*	NA
Oriole, Bullock's	*Icterus bullockii*	NA
Oriole, Orchard	*Icterus spurius*	NA
Oriole, Scott's	*Icterus parisorum*	NA
Oropendola, Chestnut-headed	*Psarocolius wagleri*	NT
Ostrich*	*Struthio camelus*	AF
Ovenbird	*Seiurus aurocapillus*	NA
Oxpecker, Red-billed	*Buphagus erythrorhynchus*	AF
Oxpecker, Yellow-billed	*Buphagus africanus*	AF
Palila	*Loxioides bailleui*	AU
Paradise-Flycatcher, African	*Terpsiphone viridis*	AF
Paradise-Flycatcher, Asian	*Terpsiphone paradisi*	OR
Paradise-Flycatcher, Madagascar	*Terpsiphone mutata*	AF
Paradise-Whydah, Northern	*Vidua orientalis*	AF
Pardalote, Spotted	*Pardalotus punctatus*	AU
Pardalote, Striated	*Pardalotus striatus*	AU
Parotia, Lawes'	*Parotia lawesii*	AU
Penduline-Tit, Cape	*Anthoscopus minutus*	AF
Penduline-Tit, European	*Remiz pendulinus*	PA
Pewee, Greater Antillean	*Contopus caribacus*	NT
Phainopepla	*Phainopepla nitens*	NA
Phoebe, Black	*Sayornis nigricans*	NA, NT
Phoebe, Eastern	*Sayornis phoebe*	NA
Piapiac	*Ptilostomus afer*	AF
Piha, Screaming	*Lipaugus vociferans*	NT
Pilotbird	*Pycnoptilus floccosus*	AU
Piopio	*Turnagra capensis*	AU
Pipit, South Georgia	*Anthus antarcticus*	NT
Pipit, Sprague's	*Anthus spragueii*	NA
Pitohui, Hooded	*Pitohui dichrous*	AU
Pitta, African	*Pitta angolensis*	AF
Pitta, Blue-banded	*Pitta arcuata*	OR
Pitta, Fairy	*Pitta nympha*	PA
Pitta, Gurney's	*Pitta gurneyi*	OR
Pitta, Noisy	*Pitta versicolor*	AU
Pitta, Red-bellied	*Pitta erythrogaster*	AU
Pitta, Superb	*Pitta superba*	AU
Plantcutter, White-tipped	*Phytotoma rutila*	NT
Ploughbill, Wattled	*Eulacestoma nigropectus*	AU
Pytilia, Green-winged	*Pytilia melba*	AF
Quelea, Red-billed	*Quelea quelea*	AF
Raven, Common	*Corvus corax*	NA, PA
Raven, Thick-billed	*Corvus crassirostris*	AF
Redpoll, Common	*Carduelis flammea*	NA, PA
Redstart, American	*Setophaga ruticilla*	NA
Redstart, Collared	*Myioborus torquatus*	NT
Reedhaunter, Curve-billed	*Limnornis curvirostris*	NT
Reedling, Bearded	*Panurus biarmicus*	PA
Riflebird, Queen Victoria's	*Ptiloris victoriae*	AU
Rifleman	*Acanthisitta chloris*	AU
Robin, American	*Turdus migratorius*	NA
Robin, European	*Erithacus rubecula*	PA
Robin, New Zealand	*Petroica australis*	AU
Robin, Rose	*Petroica rosea*	AU
Rock-Jumper, Orange-breasted	*Chaetops aurantius*	AU
Rook	*Corvus frugilegus*	PA
Rubythroat, Siberian	*Luscinia calliope*	PA
Rush-Tyrant, Many-colored	*Tachuris rubrigastra*	NT
Rushbird, Wrenlike	*Phleocryptes melanops*	NT
Scrub-Bird, Noisy	*Atrichornis clamosus*	AU
Scrub-Bird, Rufous	*Atrichornis rufescens*	AU
Seedcracker, Black-bellied	*Pyrenestes ostrinus*	AF
Serin	*Serinus serinus*	PA
Shrike, Brown	*Lanius cristatus*	PA, OR
Shrike, Loggerhead	*Lanius ludovicianus*	NA
Shrike, Long-tailed	*Lanius schach*	OR, AU
Shrike, Northern	*Lanius excubitor*	NA, PA
Shrike, Red-backed	*Lanius collurio*	PA
Shriketit, Crested	*Falcunculus frontatus*	AU
Sicklebill, Brown	*Epimachus meyeri*	AU
Sicklebill, Buff-tailed	*Epimachus albertisi*	AU
Silvereye	*Zosterops lateralis*	AU
Siskin, Red	*Carduelis cucullata*	NT
Sittella, Varied	*Daphoenositta chrysoptera*	AU
Skylark	*Alauda arvensis*	PA
Slaty-Flycatcher, Crowned	*Griseotyrannus aurantioatrocristatus*	NT
Solitaire, Slate-colored	*Myadestes unicolor*	NT
Songlark, Brown	*Cincloramphus cruralis*	AU
Sparrow, American Tree	*Spizella arborea*	NA
Sparrow, Baird's	*Ammodramus bairdii*	NA
Sparrow, Chestnut	*Passer eminibey*	AF
Sparrow, Dusky Seaside	*Ammodramus maritimus nigrescens*	NA
Sparrow, Eurasian Tree	*Passer montanus*	PA, OR
Sparrow, Five-striped	*Aimophila quinquestriata*	NA
Sparrow, Grasshopper	*Ammodramus savannarum*	NA
Sparrow, Henslow's	*Ammodramus henslowi*	NA
Sparrow, House	*Passer domesticus*	PA
Sparrow, Java	*Padda oryzivora*	OR
Sparrow, Nelson's Sharp-tailed	*Ammodramus nelsoni*	NA
Sparrow, Rufous-collared	*Zonotrichia capensis*	NT
Sparrow, Saltmarsh Sharp-tailed	*Ammodramus caudacutus*	NA
Sparrow, Savannah	*Passerculus sandwichensis*	NA
Sparrow, Seaside	*Ammodramus maritimus*	NA
Sparrow, Song	*Melospiza melodia*	NA
Sparrow, Swamp	*Melospiza georgiana*	NA
Sparrow, Vesper	*Pooecetes gramineus*	NA
Sparrow, White-crowned	*Zonotrichia leucophrys*	NA
Sparrow, White-throated	*Zonotrichia albicollis*	NA

Spinetail, Pale-breasted	*Synallaxis albescens*	NT
Starling, European	*Sturnus vulgaris*	PA
Starling, Pale-winged	*Onychognathus nabouroup*	AF
Starling, Red-winged	*Onychognathus morio*	AF
Starling, Rosy	*Sturnus roseus*	PA
Starling, Wattled	*Creatophora cinerea*	AF
Stitchbird	*Notiomystis cincta*	AU
Sugarbird, Gurney's	*Promerops gurneyi*	AF
Sunbird, Golden-winged	*Nectarinia reichenowi*	AF
Sunbird, Malachite	*Nectarinia famosa*	AF
Sunbird, Scarlet-tufted Malachite	*Nectarinia johnstoni*	AF
Sunbird, Variable	*Nectarinia venusta*	AF
Sunbird-Asity, Common	*Neodrepanis coruscans*	AF
Swallow, Bank (see Martin, Sand)		
Swallow, Barn	*Hirundo rustica*	all regions
Swallow, Black Saw-wing	*Psalidoprocne holomelas*	AF
Swallow, Chilean	*Tachycineta meyeni*	NT
Swallow, Cliff	*Hirundo pyrrhonota*	NA
Swallow, South African Cliff	*Hirundo spilodera*	AF
Swallow, Tree	*Tachycineta bicolor*	NA
Tanager, Black-crowned Palm	*Phaenicophilus palmarum*	NT
Tanager, Scarlet	*Piranga olivacea*	NA
Tanager, Stripe-headed	*Spindalis zena*	NT
Tanager, Summer	*Piranga rubra*	NA
Tern, Sooty*	*Sterna fuscata*	all regions
Thornbird, Rufous-fronted	*Phacellodomus rufifrons*	NT
Thrasher, Brown	*Toxostoma rufum*	NA
Thrasher, Le Conte's	*Toxostoma lecontei*	NA
Thrush, Bicknell's	*Catharus bicknelli*	NA
Thrush, Gray-cheeked	*Catharus minimus*	NA
Thrush, Hermit	*Catharus guttatus*	NA
Thrush, Lawrence's	*Turdus lawrencii*	NT
Thrush, Song	*Turdus philomelos*	PA
Thrush, Swainson's	*Catharus ustulatus*	NA
Thrush, Tristan	*Nesocichla eremita*	NT
Thrush, Varied	*Zoothera naevia*	NA
Thrush, Wood	*Catharus mustelinus*	NA
Tit, Blue	*Parus caeruleus*	PA
Tit, Coal	*Parus ater*	PA
Tit, Crested	*Parus cristatus*	PA
Tit, Great	*Parus major*	PA
Tit, Long-tailed	*Aegithalos caudatus*	PA
Tit, Marsh	*Parus palustris*	PA
Tit, Pygmy	*Psaltria exilis*	PA
Tit, Siberian (Gray-headed Chickadee)	*Parus cinctus*	NA, PA
Towhee, California	*Pipilo crissalis*	NA
Towhee, Canyon	*Pipilo fuscus*	NA
Treecreeper, Brown	*Climacteris picumnus*	AU
Treecreeper, European	*Certhia familiaris*	NA
Treecreeper, White-throated	*Cormobates leucophaea*	AU
Treerunner, Ruddy	*Margarornis rubiginosus*	NT
Treerunner, White-throated	*Pygarrhichas albogularis*	NT
Triller, White-winged	*Lalage sueurii*	AU
Troupial	*Icterus icterus*	NT
Tuftedcheek, Buffy	*Pseudocolaptes lawrencii*	NT
Tui	*Prosthemadera novaeseelandiae*	AU
Tyrant, Cattle	*Machetornis rixosus*	NT
Tyrant, Chocolate-vented	*Neoxolmis rufiventris*	NT
Tyrant, Cock-tailed	*Alectrurus tricolor*	NT
Tyrant, Strange-tailed	*Alectrurus risora*	NT
Tyrant, Streamer-tailed	*Gubernetes yetapa*	NT
Tyrant, Yellow-browed	*Satrapa icterophrys*	NT
Ula-ai-hawane	*Ciridops anna*	AU
Umbrellabird, Bare-necked	*Cephalopterus glabricollis*	NT
Vanga, Blue	*Cyanolanius madagascarinus*	AF
Vanga, Helmet	*Euryceros prevostii*	AF
Vanga, Nuthatch	*Hypositta corallirostris*	AF
Vanga, Sickle-billed	*Falculea palliata*	AF
Verdin	*Auriparus flaviceps*	NA
Vireo, Black-capped	*Vireo atricapillus*	NA
Vireo, Blue Mountain	*Vireo osburni*	NT
Vireo, Philadelphia	*Vireo philadelphicus*	NA
Vireo, Red-eyed	*Vireo olivaceus*	NA
Vireo, Warbling	*Vireo gilvus*	NA
Vulture, Turkey*	*Cathartes aura*	NA, NT
Wagtail, White	*Motacilla alba*	NA, PA
Wagtail, Yellow	*Motacilla flava*	NA, PA
Wallcreeper	*Tichodroma muraria*	PA
Warbler, Aquatic	*Acrocephalus paludicola*	PA
Warbler, Arctic	*Phylloscopus borealis*	NA, PA
Warbler, Bachman's	*Vermivora bachmanii*	NA
Warbler, Bay-breasted	*Dendroica castanea*	NA
Warbler, Black-and-white	*Mniotilta varia*	NA
Warbler, Black-throated Blue	*Dendroica caerulescens*	NA
Warbler, Black-throated Green	*Dendroica virens*	NA
Warbler, Blackburnian	*Dendroica fusca*	NA
Warbler, Blackpoll	*Dendroica striata*	NA
Warbler, Blue-winged	*Vermivora pinus*	NA
Warbler, Canada	*Wilsonia canadensis*	NA
Warbler, Cape May	*Dendroica tigrina*	NA
Warbler, Cerulean	*Dendroica cerulea*	NA
Warbler, Cetti's	*Cettia cetti*	PA
Warbler, Chestnut-sided	*Dendroica pensylvanica*	NA
Warbler, Connecticut	*Oporornis agilis*	NA
Warbler, Cryptic	*Cryptosylvicola randrianasoloi*	AF
Warbler, Garden	*Sylvia borin*	PA
Warbler, Golden-winged	*Vermivora chrysoptera*	NA
Warbler, Great Reed	*Acrocephalus arundinaceus*	PA

Warbler, Henderson Island Reed	*Acrocephalus taiti*	AU
Warbler, Hooded	*Wilsonia citrina*	NA
Warbler, Kentucky	*Oporornis formosus*	NA
Warbler, Kirtland's	*Dendroica kirtlandii*	NA
Warbler, Marsh	*Acrocephalus palustris*	PA
Warbler, Moustached	*Acrocephalus melanopogon*	PA
Warbler, Prothonotary	*Protonotaria citrea*	NA
Warbler, Reed	*Acrocephalus scirpaceus*	PA
Warbler, Sedge	*Acrocephalus schoenobaenus*	PA
Warbler, Swainson's	*Limnothlypis swainsonii*	NA
Warbler, Tahiti Reed	*Acrocephalus caffer*	AU
Warbler, Willow	*Phylloscopus trochilus*	PA
Warbler, Wood	*Phylloscopus sibilatrix*	PA
Warbler, Worm-eating	*Helmitheros vermivorus*	NA
Warbler, Yellow	*Dendroica petechia*	NA
Warbler, Yellow-browed	*Phylloscopus inornatus*	PA
Warbler, Yellow-rumped	*Dendroica coronata*	NA
Water-Redstart, Plumbeous	*Rhyacornis fuliginosus*	PA, OR
Water-Redstart, White-capped	*Chaimarrornis leucocephalus*	PA, OR
Waterthrush, Louisiana	*Seiurus motacilla*	NA
Wattlebird, Red	*Anthochaera carunculata*	AU
Waxwing, Bohemian	*Bombycilla garrulus*	NA, PA
Waxwing, Cedar	*Bombycilla cedrorum*	NA
Weaver, Baya	*Ploceus philippinus*	OR
Weaver, Black-breasted	*Ploceus benghalensis*	OR
Weaver, Parasitic	*Anomalospiza imberbis*	AF
Weaver, Social	*Philetairus socius*	AF
Weaver, Streaked	*Ploceus manyar*	OR
Weaver, Village	*Ploceus cucullatus*	AF
Wheatear, Northern	*Oenanthe oenanthe*	NA, PA
Whipbird, Eastern	*Psophodes olivaceus*	AU
White-eye, Bridled	*Zosterops conspicillatus*	AU
White-eye, Lord Howe Island	*Zosterops tephropleurus*	AU
Whitethroat, Common	*Sylvia communis*	PA
Whitethroat, Lesser	*Sylvia curruca*	PA
Whydah, Shaft-tailed	*Vidua regia*	AF
Whydah, Straw-tailed	*Vidua fischeri*	AF
Widowbird, Jackson's	*Euplectes jacksoni*	AF
Widowbird, Long-tailed	*Euplectes progne*	AF
Widowbird, Yellow-shouldered	*Euplectes macrourus*	AF
Wood-Pewee, Eastern	*Contopus virens*	NA
Wood-Pewee, Western	*Contopus sordidulus*	NA
Woodswallow, Black-faced	*Artamus cinereus*	AU
Woodswallow, Masked	*Artamus personatus*	AU
Wren, Bewick's	*Thryomanes bewickii*	NA
Wren, Blue (see Fairy-Wren, Superb)		
Wren, Bush	*Xenicus longipes*	AU
Wren, Cactus	*Campylorhynchus brunneicapillus*	NA
Wren, Carolina	*Thryothorus ludovicianus*	NA
Wren, House	*Troglodytes aedon*	NA, NT
Wren, Marsh	*Cistothorus palustris*	NA
Wren, New Zealand Rock	*Xenicus gilviventris*	AU
Wren, Rock	*Salpinctes obsoletus*	AU
Wren, Rufous-breasted	*Thryothorus rutilus*	NT
Wren, Sedge	*Cistothorus platensis*	NA, NT
Wren, Stephens Island	*Xenicus lyalli*	AU
Wren, Winter	*Troglodytes troglodytes*	NA, PA
Wrenthrush	*Zeledonia coronata*	NT
Yellowhammer	*Emberiza citrinella*	PA

*not a songbird

GENERAL INDEX